GREAT GAMES!

Old & New, Indoor/Outdoor, Travel, Board, Ball & Word

Sam Taggar

with Susan Williamson

Illustrations by
Michael Kline

Williamson Publishing • Charlotte, Vermont

Library of Congress Cataloging-in-Publication Data

Taggar, Sam.
Great Games! : old & new, indoor/outdoor, travel, board, ball & word / Sam Taggar & Susan Williamson ; illustrations by Michael Kline.
    p. cm.
    "A Williamson kids can! book."
    Summary: A collection of indoor and outdoor games—including tag games, board games, ball games, neighborhood games, word games, and more—with tips on how to choose who goes first and game-playing strategies.
    ISBN 1-885593-72-4 (pbk.)
    1. Games--Juvenile literature. [1. Games.] I. Kline, Michael P., ill. II. Title.

GV1203.T32 2004
793--dc21

                                                        2002191007

Kids Can!® series editor: Susan Williamson
Cover design and illustrations: Michael Kline
Interior design: Sarah Rakitin
Interior illustrations: Michael Kline
Project coordinator: Jean Silveira
Research: Emily Stetson, Dana Pierson
Printing: Quebecor World

Williamson Publishing Co.
P.O. Box 185
Charlotte, VT 05445
(800) 234-8791

Printed in Canada

10 9 8 7 6 5 4 3 2 1

Other Williamson Publishing books that you may enjoy:

Summer Fun! by Susan Williamson
Boredom Busters! by Avery Hart and Paul Mantell
Kids Make Music! by Avery Hart and Paul Mantell
Kids Art Works! by Sandi Henry
Kids Cook! by Sarah Williamson and Zachary Williamson

(Please see last page for how to order these and other great books.)

....

Trademark references and acknowledgments:
Games that do not appear with a trademark symbol or are not acknowledged below may have trademark status.

Balderdash is a registered trademark of Gameworks Creations

Battleship, Scrabble, and *Yahtzee* are registered trademarks of Milton Bradley

Pick-Up-Sticks is a registered trademark of Rose Art Industries

Pictionary is a registered trademark of Western Publishing Company

Parker Brothers is referenced as the producer of many games including, but not limited to *Clue* and *Monopoly.*

We gratefully acknowledge a wonderful resource on games, *The Games Treasury* by Merilyn Simonds Mohr, published by Chapters. When we faced too many variations to a game, we turned to this large collection as the final arbiter.

For Jack

· · · · · · · · · ·

A heartfelt thanks to my colleagues who worked their magic and staid the course 'til this project was completed with style, integrity, and good spirit. Special thanks to Emily Stetson, who loves games at least as much as I do and contributed so much to this book; to Sarah Rakitin, whose lively design once again restored order while keeping the spirit of the book alive; to Mike Kline whose clever illustrations always remind me of the importance of collaboration among writer, illustrator, designer, and editor; to Jean Silveira, who not only puts the stamp of excellence on all of our books, but does so while managing a myriad of other responsibilities; to Vicky Congdon who quietly worked away on other projects so I could focus on this, and to Dana Pierson who would have had this book done long ago and on time.

To my game-playing family: Jack, Sarah, and Zachary Williamson; Elaine, Paul, Rachel, and Dan Dratch; Jane Soloway, Mitch Moody, and Jonathan Moody; Debby, Stan, Joelle, and David Sobin; and Linda, Bruce, Ashley, Ryan, and Whitney Williamson. And to my Park Avenue friends: Jean Vincent, Pam Moore, Kay Carroll, Lynne Vincent, Jean Saberski, and Jane Terrill. To some very special Vermont game players: Erin, Annie, and Laura Jackson, Andrew and Wayne Miller, Adrienne Vail, and Greg Campbell. Thank you all!

Table of Contents

GOTCHA! TAG GAMES! 77

PLAY BALL! 84

MULTICULTURAL GAMES 106

Multicultural Board Games & Other Assorted Fun 107

Ball, Tag & Other Active Games . . 121

Index 125

Gamesmanship Is the Name of the Game!

Hi, all of you game players! Please allow me to introduce myself: Sam Taggar, a kid who never grew up when it comes to games of every description, and also a lover of kids (big, little, older, younger, teens, tweens, and their 'rents), family, friends, dogs, and fun times. I am thrilled to be sharing with you some of the all-time best-ever most-loved games, as voted on by a group of my friends, family, Susan, Emily, and me. OK, so it's not a very scientific study that you'll find here. I like to think of it more as a measure of enthusiastic recollections and current favorites, sort of like having a game applause-o-meter.

Sam says... **First thing, find the best way to make this book work for you.** I expect it to become dog-eared from all the times you need to look something up in it, and that's just fine. After all, a book is only as good as what you get out of it! So, here's how you can use this one:

✳ Skim through the table of contents to see what kinds of games interest you. Then, skim through that section to find a game you'd like to play.

✳ Read the book to find out about games you never heard of that you think you might enjoy, plus find new ways to play old favorites.

✳ If you know what you are looking for, then use the index on pages 125 to 127 to:

  ✳ look up games by **number of players**

  ✳ look up **types of games**: ball, board, tag, travel, word, etc.

  ✳ look up by **site**

  ✳ look up by **game name**, but remember: Most games have several different names

Try something new, play something old, introduce someone to one of your favorites, get a little exercise for your body and your brain, and change the rules to suit you and your buddies.

But most of all, have fun — lots of it!

It's not whether you win or lose, But how you play the game!

Uh-oh, one of those quotes. (See, I know what you are thinking because I'm still very much a kid at heart.) No, this isn't going to be a lecture, despite that saying, but as you'll soon realize, everyone who truly enjoys playing games cannot tolerate whiners, bullies, controllers, and cheaters. Why? Because they spoil everyone's fun, make people feel grumpy, and just sort of don't get why we're playing the game in the first place.

Gamesmanship — just like sportsmanship, only used when playing games — is a very important part of game tradition. I bet you can already guess how I feel about gamesmanship: It is more important than the game itself, just like that old-time saying states.

Now, you might think that winning is the main idea, and in competitive play, it sure does motivate people to do their best. But when someone cheats or bullies others in order to win, well, that person is a loser, no matter what the final score is. Besides, when you are playing with someone who only thinks about winning, the game isn't much fun. The other players often walk away muttering to themselves, or feeling frustrated. That isn't what any game is supposed to do. After a game, if everyone has played fairly, all the players should feel good! And, best of all, everyone will want to play together the next time.

Sam says:

10 WAYS TO KEEP GAMES FAIR & FUN

GREAT GAME!

* SAFETY FIRST! Choose where you play carefully and look out for the safety of all players — including those on the opposing team.

* Decide on the rules *before* the game begins.

* If there is a judge or an umpire, all players and all teams must agree that the judge's call is final.

* Players shake hands before the game begins.

* Give a team cheer to build team spirit.

* Do compete; don't cheat!

* Don't bully or make fun of other players — EVER!

* Compliment your opponents when they make a good move or good play! The best game players appreciate skill — even in their opponents!

* Complete the game by doing your best, even if you are getting trounced! (Try not to get moody or down on yourself.)

* Accept defeat graciously, without placing blame on anyone.

* Shake your opponent's hand, while you congratulate her.

No Place to Play?

I was lucky as a kid because I lived in a small town where kids could play in people's yards, at the park, or at the school ball fields. Finding a safe place to play was never a problem. The world has changed since then, and now some parks are not safe for kids, adult supervision is needed for just about everything, most people do not have big yards, and the school ball fields are busy with after-school sports. What's a game-lovin' person to do?

Use your game-playing strategy to seek out possible places to play! First, before you do anything, assess the situation. Be sure to consider these points, especially as they relate to where you live, how old you and your friends are, and how rambunctious you all are likely to become in your games.

* **Safety:** Is there traffic? Are strangers loitering about?
* **Trespassing:** Yes, I know you are a good kid, but you always need permission — even from your own folks and, of course, from neighbors. Every time.
* **Logistics:** So you've come up with the perfect place, but, uh, how are you going to get there?

If you are trying to use a public space or a privately owned business space, then add these to your considerations:

* **Supervision:** Most places will insist on adult supervision.
* **Timing:** Will you want to play at the same time the building is usually in use?
* **Reliability:** Are you and your friends capable of following all of the rules, if you get permission to play somewhere?
* **Bartering:** Be prepared to offer something in return for using a space, such as setting up chairs for meetings, mowing the lawn, or weeding the landscaping.

A Little Bartering ...

Here are some suggestions for how to find a really great place to play, indoors and out, all year long:

✱ **Ask a group of parents** to bring you and your buddies to a safe park, a few times a week, taking turns supervising.

✱ If you live in an apartment or condo association, **ask the superintendent or the owner of the building** where you can play safely. In exchange, offer to clean up some area.

✱ **Ask the school principal or the superintendent** if there are times over the weekend when the school is open, so you can either use the playground or an indoor gym to play. A lot of gyms and playgrounds are locked after school and on weekends. (Now, that is sure a waste of good game-playing spaces!) Make an appointment to speak with the person in charge. Bring along a list of what you would like to do, and when, where, and who will supervise you. Offer to do something in exchange, such as set up chairs for a big meeting.

✱ **Ask the town clerk, mayor, selectboard, or neighborhood association for the same permission**, especially if the town hall has a big yard or big hall. Be prepared to barter.

✱ **Ask any churches, synagogues, mosques, and other meeting places for religious groups** if you can use their open halls or yards. (Don't worry; you won't have to be a follower of that religion to play there.)

✱ **If there is an empty lot on your street or nearby, get permission from the landowner** to clean it up. These "pocket parks" are wonderful neighborhood places for everyone! This will involve help from adults, too, so plan a cleanup day when lots of people can pitch in. Put up fliers, and don't forget to ask older people, even if they don't have kids around anymore. Most times, they'd love to get involved.

If this sounds like a lot more work than you bargained for, just think of this: Your efforts to make spaces available for indoor and outdoor games may allow you to play there for many years to come. Awesome! Now, let's get this (game) show on the road!

OVER HERE!

One Potato, Two Potato...
Plus other ways to choose "It" and Teams

OK, I know there is always someone who insists on being first, or "It," or on deciding what to play. And, sure enough, there is always someone else who never wants to be first, never wants to be "It," and doesn't care what we play. What's a kid who just wants to have FUN supposed to do?

Beginning a game doesn't have to be a declaration of war, you know. It can be as much fun as playing the game itself. Plus, it can involve some very silly rhymes that become even sillier when you all make up your own verses.

These are some of my favorite choosing "It" methods. So — as people who love games always say — "Quit your talkin' and let's play!"

A Game Before the Games

The choosing of "It" can be a game in itself. This is especially true if everyone will just relax a little, keeping in mind that, hey dudes, we're here to share some time and fun with our friends! Nothing more and nothing less.

So form a small circle and ask everyone to put one fist into the center. You begin a "choosing rhyme," bouncing your fist gently around the circle, landing on the next fist with each word. (Start at your right and land on your own fist last.)

The most common way to do the choosing is to have the last person "fisted" in the rhyme be "It." In some versions, the words in the rhyme actually do the choosing: *My mother says to pick the very best one, and you are "It"!* So the last one pointed to is "It."

Or, add to the end of any rhyme: *O-U-T spells out, so out you must go.* The person who is "go" is out of the circle, and the rhyme continues until only one person is left. Guess who that is? Ta-da — "It"!

Before you play the games, become a true-blue rhymin' machine!

One potato, two potato, three potato, four,
Five potato, six potato, seven potato, more.
Acha-bacha, cuca-racha, out goes Y-O-U!

Eeny, meeny, miney, mo
Catch a hedgehog by the toe,
If it hollers, let it go
Eeny, meeny, miney, mo.
My mother says to choose the very best one,
And that's Y-O-U spells YOU!

Inka-dink a bottle of ink,
The cork fell out and you stink;
Not because you're dirty,
Not because you're clean,
Just because ya kissed a (say, "guy" or "gal")
Behind a magazine.

Ink blotter,
One-zum, two-zum, zick-zum, zam!
Pop-tail vinegar tickler tam
Am scam boozaler bam
Oliver, boliver, blue,
Out goes YOU!

Bubble gum, bubble gum in a dish
How many pieces do you wish?
(Person pointed to says a number, say, "three")
Three? One, two, three, and out you go
With your uncle's big fat toe!

My sister and your sister
Talk every day.
Every time they have a chat
This is what they say,
"Ickabacker, ickabacker, ickabacker, boo!
ickabacker, soda cracker, out goes Y-O-U!"

My mother and your mother were hanging out clothes,
When along came Billy with a bloody nose.
What color was his blood?
R-E-D spells red!

(Or, add)
My mother says to pick this very one ...
And you are "It"!

Blue shoe, blue shoe,
How old are you?
(The last person "fisted" tells his age, and the rhymer counts it out on the fists. Last one fisted steps out.)

One, two,
Sky blue,
All out,
Beginning with you!

Engine, engine, number nine,
Going down Chicago line.
If the train falls off the track,
Do you want your money back?
The player whose fist is hit on the word "back" can answer "yes" or "no." The rhymer then spells out the answer:

N-O spells no
or
Y-E-S spells yes.
The person who is fisted on "yes" or "no" steps out.

Rock, Paper, Scissors

Kids in Japan sometimes choose "It" with a traditional game called *Jan-Ken-Pon* (john-kehn-pone). We call it ROCK, PAPER, SCISSORS.

To play, two or three players hold one hand behind their backs and at the count of *One, two, three!* bring their hands forward in one of the three positions shown.

Scissors can cut *paper* and so becomes the winner, but *Paper* can wrap around (and beat) *Rock*; yet, *Rock* smashes the *Scissors*.

You can actually play this as a game in itself!

ROCK
(a fist)

PAPER
(a flat palm)

SCISSORS
(two fingers pointing sideways, in a V, like scissors)

Choosing Teams

Show me a person who doesn't like to play games, and I'll show you a person who has had a bad experience when it comes to choosing teams. Well, truth is, those experiences really do hurt people's feelings — no doubt about it. The good news is that teams can be selected without anyone getting hurt feelings and with the teams evenly balanced, too.

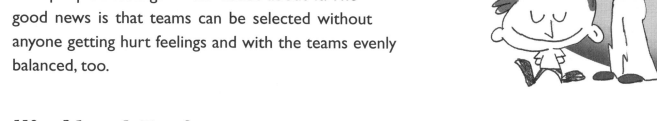

It's About Fun!

For one thing, no one has fun if one team is selected to tilt the balance unfairly: A certain skill is loaded up on one team; all the younger kids are playing against all the older kids; or the loudest person wants all his friends on his team, causing others to feel left out. A good team has some of every kind of person, just like a good game involves many kinds of skills — and you can quote me on that! After all, you may be a slow runner, but you have the best strategies of anyone, young or old. So when picking teams, do the right thing: Pick someone you don't know, or someone who looks a little bewildered, or someone who is sort of hanging back. If your team wins, well, that is nice, but even if it doesn't, you will be a winner, probably have a lot of fun, and meet some nice people you didn't know before, too.

OK, now you know who is "It" and the different types of skills the players bring to your team, so you are ready to let the great games begin!

Just a Few of Us!

To my way of thinking, nothing beats hanging out with a couple of friends on the weekend or during vacation. What could be better, I ask you? I like to get my chores done early in the day so I am pretty much free to use the rest of the day as I want. Often we just toss a ball around for a few hours, maybe bake some cookies or concoct a big lunch, and listen to some tunes. But then, we get involved in some of these great games. No big productions, no expensive equipment, just us having fun! You gotta love it!

With any of these games, if you would like a fun way to decide who goes first, there are lots to choose from on pages 12 to 15. For more games that are perfect for two to four players, please see Phun with Werds, pages 65 to 76, and the index, pages 125 to 127.

STICK? THIS IS A KID-COMPATIBLE, SELF-CONTAINED, TIMBERED DIRT DIVIDER AND GAME-DELINEATING DEVICE.

A Ball, a Stone, and Us!

These games require one to four players, and maybe a piece of white chalk to draw the lines on pavement or a stick for in the dirt. They probably have been played by many generations (did you know that a generation is about 20 years?) and some are said to have been played in ancient times.

What makes these games so awesome to me is that, as old as some of them are, kids of all ages still love playing them today. People may call them by different names and play them with slightly different rules and variations, but wherever you visit or move to — even to a new country across the ocean! — you'll find kids who play them. These games are like old friends that introduce you to new friends. Now that is just so cool!

UP AGAINST

I think this is probably the game that my buddies and I played most often when we were just together, hanging out. We never actually thought of it as a game, because we just sort of played while we were talking about other stuff. It isn't really competitive and it doesn't take any endurance, but it is somehow compelling and lots of fun. All of us were super good at this because it is also the game that we practiced most by ourselves. It's hard to describe what the appeal is, but beware — it can be habit-forming!

* **PLAYERS:** 1 to about 4 work best

* **AGES:** About 8 and older

* **SITE:** Best played outdoors where there is a flat, paved surface (packed gravel or dirt works, too) and a flat wall or chimney to play against, or indoors in a basement with similar surfaces (and permission)

* **MATERIALS:** Tennis or Pinky ball

* **GOALS:** To complete a preselected set of Stumpers

* **NOTE:** Stumpers are described on pages 19 to 20

Let's Play

The play: Whether alone or taking turns, play a preselected set of Stumpers in order. Each Stumper must be done as many times as the number you are on (so for Stumper #7 you have to do it seven times). Play is usually to 10 or 12 Stumpers.

Rules/scoring: Always begin on Stumper #1, because if you miss, you have to go back to #1. Misses include not catching the ball on one bounce, not completing the Stumper before catching the ball, and stepping out-of-bounds (if you play with boundaries).

To win: The first player to complete the 10 or 12 Stumpers is the winner.

Variations: Some people play that you add an extra move, such as touching the ground, to each Stumper once you complete the whole set. You can then make it increasingly difficult with each next set, such as next touching the ground *and* patting your head while doing all the Stumpers. And so on.

SUPER UP AGAINST: To make the game more difficult, play that you are not allowed to let the ball bounce when tossed against the wall.

People call these tricks by all different names — Stumpers, Challenges, Stumblers, Mimsies, or Fancies are the ones I've heard most. Whatever they are called, they are used to make the game more challenging and lots more fun! The ones listed here can be used in BOXBALL (page 22), UP AGAINST (page 18), "A" MY NAME IS ALICE (page 21), and a myriad of other games that ask you to do increasingly difficult moves. Most Stumpers work, with slight variations, in games where you are bouncing a ball on the ground, throwing it up in the air and doing the Stumper before it hits the ground, or throwing it against a wall and letting it bounce once.

LEG-CLAP

UNDER-LEG

✳ *Hop* on one foot (on a BOXBALL course, you roll the ball and then hop through the course to get to it and continue to the baseline).

✳ *Skip* (on a BOXBALL course)

✳ *Clap-through:* Clap your hands while bouncing the ball with the ball going "through" the clap, as many times as required without pausing (no wall toss for this).

✳ *Leg-over* a.k.a. *O'Leary* (as in ONE, TWO, THREE O'LEARY): Can do right leg going over the ball to the right, then going to the left, and left leg going to the left, then going to the right. (Just so you know, *a.k.a.* means "also known as.")

✳ *Front-back-front clap:* Clap once in front, once in back, and then once in front again while the ball is bouncing, in the air, or against the wall.

✳ *Under-leg:* Toss or bounce from under your leg. Once tossed, you need to catch it without a bounce.

✳ *Leg-clap:* Clap under your raised leg while bouncing, in the air, or against the wall.

✳ *Triple-clap raised leg:* Clap over, under, and over your raised leg before the ball bounces.

JUMPING JACK

SCHOOL NURSE

ME, TARZAN

* *Jump Sally:* Jump down, touch the ground, and turn around before the ball bounces.

* *Jumping jack:* Clap over your head as part of doing a jumping jack.

* *Bouncies:* Toss the ball and let it bounce.

* *No bouncies:* Toss the ball, catching it before it bounces.

* *Toss & turn:* Toss the ball and turn around, letting the ball bounce once.

* *No bouncies toss & turn:* Toss the ball and turn around, catching it before it bounces.

* *Double twist:* Do at least two twists before the ball bounces.

* *Shoulder toss:* Toss the ball over your shoulder in the air or at the wall, then turn to catch it.

* *School nurse:* Touch your head, tug on your ear, pretend to blow your nose, and hold your tummy before the ball bounces.

* *Turkey trot:* Poke your hands into your armpits and strut before catching the ball.

* *Barnyard:* Flap your "wings" and either cluck like a chicken, neigh like a horse, moo like a cow, or oink like a pig twice before catching the ball.

* *School spirit:* Do a "cheerleader" jump (arms out, legs spread) while saying *Go, Team, Go!* before catching the ball.

* *Me, Tarzan* or *Me, Jane:* Give Tarzan's jungle call and pound on your chest three times before catching the ball.

Z my name is ZELDA, My husband's name is ZACHARY, We live in ZIMBABWE, and we sell ZEBRAS!

We love UP AGAINST. We almost always play with a set of the same Stumpers every time. Stumper #8 is always *triple-clap raised leg* and #9 is always *leg over*, which we do on numbers 3, 6, and 9 while bouncing the ball nine times. You'd think it would get boring, but it never does. My older sister used to play this, and to this day, when she sees a Pinky ball, she's got to find a wall to play UP AGAINST!

— Debby

"A" My Name Is Alice

Quick Takes

Using the alphabet poem below, you take a turn going as far through the alphabet as you can, while doing a *leg over* every time you say an alphabet word. You must keep the ball bouncing in a steady rhythm and do the *leg overs,* and you need to use real words, names, and places for every letter. When you miss or hesitate (only one bounce on the alphabet-word), you lose your turn. You can play that you get to continue on your next turn or must begin again. The winner is the first person to get through the whole alphabet or whoever gets furthest.

PASS THE P'S PLEASE: One person begins with A, doing as above, and then the person to her right must begin on B, and so on around the group. If you miss, hesitate, or change the rhythm, you must step out, and the next person picks up quickly. The winner is the last player standing. So much fun with two people and more fun with more!

A my name is ALICE, my husband's name is AL,
We live in ALABAMA and we sell APPLES.

B my name is BOBBY, my wife's name is BARB,
We live in BERMUDA and we sell BUGS.

C my name is CAROL, my husband's name is CARL,
We live in COLORADO and we sell CRABS.

BOXBALL

This is a game that my sisters, my friends, and I have always loved — we could play it for hours at a time! It is a great game to play on a covered porch on a rainy day. I used to play by myself, trying to never make a mistake, which, I learned, was impossible!

* **PLAYERS:** 1 to about 4 work best
* **AGES:** 7 and up
* **SITE:** Best played outdoors on a flat, paved area, away from a road
* **MATERIALS:** White chalk (for lines) and a tennis or Pinky ball
* **GOAL:** To complete the course using all the Stumpers. More difficult than it looks!
* **TYKES:** Not appropriate, but you can simplify the game. Ask the child to stand in each box and then you roll the ball to her. Then switch positions.
* **NOTE:** Stumpers can be found on pages 19 to 20

The setup: Draw the course as shown here, using either six or eight squares. These squares are bigger than in HOPSCOTCH, about 3 feet x 3 feet (1 x 1 m) per square. Use a yardstick (meterstick), if you have one handy.

The play: Each player on his first turn completes the course using the basic style: Stand at the baseline; roll the ball into Box 1, walk into that box (only one foot in any box at a time), and pick up the rolling ball before it leaves the box. Then bounce the ball in that box and once in each box around the course, using only one step for each box. Repeat, rolling to Box 2, bouncing the ball two times, and so on. Each player begins with the basic style and follows any Stumpers that have already been introduced. Players pick up where they left off on their next turn.

OKAY, THIS TIME YOU HAVE TO PAT YOUR HEAD TWICE, SPIN AROUND 3 TIMES, AND WRITE AN ESSAY ON WHY YOU LIKE TO PLAY WITH ME!

BOXBALL COURT

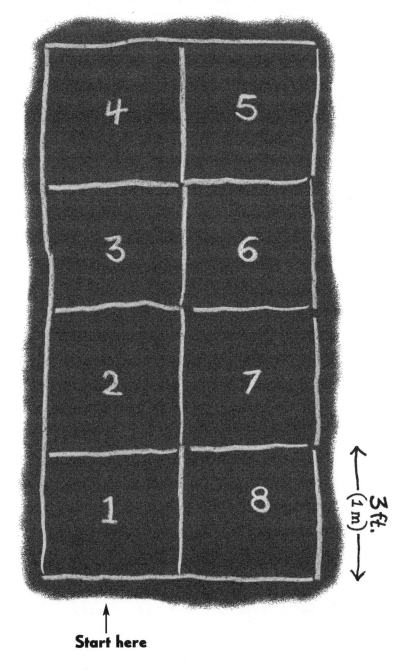

4	5
3	6
2	7
1	8

3 ft. (1 m)

↑
Start here

Rules/scoring:

✳ Continue your turn through all boxes, and then go on to introduce Stumpers, until you either step on lines, roll the ball out-of-bounds, or miss a Stumper.

✳ The first person to complete the basic course by rolling and retrieving the ball gets to select the first Stumper. Everyone who follows must use the Stumpers in the order they were determined. So, if Player 2 completes a Stumper that Player 1 chose but didn't complete, then Player 2 gets to pick the next Stumper.

✳ Every time you complete a Stumper, you get to roll your ball into the box of your choosing. If you get there before the ball goes out-of-bounds, then you can mark off any quarter of the box and put your initials in it. Only you can step in that portion.

✳ Stumpers usually pertain to the box you are in. So in *clap-through* or *leg-over*, for example, you would do the Stumper the number of times as the box you are in, and then once in every other box that you step in on the rest of the course.

To win: The first player to complete an agreed-upon number of Stumpers, or when play stops, the player with the most initialed spaces wins.

CARD FLIP

If you collect any kind of cards — baseball, soccer, basketball, skiers, Olympians — then this is a great way to have fun playing a game and also to get rid of your doubles and pick up some new faces. I mostly use baseball cards, because I always have a lot of doubles.

* **PLAYERS:** 2 or 3
* **AGES:** 8 and up
* **SITE:** Best played outdoors against a wall, stoop, or stairs, but works fine indoors, too, without carpet
* **MATERIALS:** Collecting cards
* **GOAL:** To flip your card so it touches another

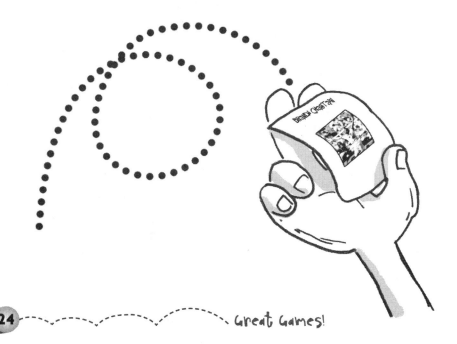

Let's Play

The setup: Play where you can stand about 8 feet (2.5 m) away from a wall, stoop, or stairs. Mark a baseline, so players don't begin creeping forward on their flip. There should not be any grass against the wall and you should be protected from the wind. Decide how many turns you each get in a game or set a time limit for play to avoid having someone leave who has won the card he wanted or because he is losing.

The play: On your turn, hold a card between your thumb, and your pointer and middle fingers, so it is facing you, bending the card slightly. Then flick your wrist and let it go: It will fly and flutter to the ground. (Another good way to flip cards is to use the same hand position you use in the HOPSCOTCH toss, page 27.) You'll eventually learn to aim and gauge how much to bend the card before you flip it. Take turns flipping cards, one card each per turn, saying *the name on the card and the team.* Pay attention so you know where the cards you want fall.

Rules/scoring: If your card lands on top of or touching another card or several cards, you get to pick up and keep those cards, leaving behind the cards that it didn't touch. Continue until you miss. Keep score by counting the cards that you win!

To win: At the end of the agreed-upon rounds, the player with the most cards won is the winner.

Variations:

✳ Your flipped card must land facing up to count as a winner, even if facedown it is touching other cards.

✳ You need to correctly point out at least one of the cards you are going to touch before you flip. Otherwise, you don't win any of the touched cards.

✳ You need to "call" a team name before flipping. Then, if you land touching any player from that team, you are a winner.

✳ If your flipped card lands faceup and standing up, you win two extra points.

✳ If your card lands touching four other cards, you win two extra points.

Easy does it! If you are a serious card collector, you need to keep it cool while playing this game. Don't expect to win some fantastic card that you always wanted, because chances are that if someone actually has that card, they probably want to keep it. Usually people who play this keep their prized cards at home, which is a very good idea. To make it more challenging for yourself, try to win cards from your favorite team or only players who all play the same position by listening to what people are flipping.

KIDS SPEAK! I never had a lot of collecting cards. I don't know why. I guess they never really interested me and I liked to collect coins instead. So when everyone played CARD FLIP, that meant I was out of the game. At first I acted as a judge, deciding if a card was really touching and stuff. Then my three buddies each gave me five cards that they had "dupes" of for me to use. From those 15 cards I gradually got enough to play with them and we took turns being judge. I still think of it as one of the nicest things anyone ever did for me.

— A grandpa remembering when he was a kid

HOPSCOTCH

There are so many ways to play HOPSCOTCH that I won't even begin to tell you all of them. Here are a couple of my favorites. This game takes some skill, but is also a matter, I believe, of having the perfect hopscotch stone.

✳ HOPSCOTCH BASICS ✳

✳ **PLAYERS:** 1 or more (great to play against yourself)

✳ **AGES:** About 7 and up, but older kids get really good at this

✳ **SITE:** Need to draw the "board" with chalk or a stick in the dirt, so either outdoors on pavement or dirt, or indoors in a basement with cement floor (with permission)

✳ **MATERIALS:** White chalk (for pavement) or stick (for dirt); hopscotch stone

✳ **GOAL:** To complete the course, keeping you and the stone where they are supposed to be and inside the lines

✳ **TYKES:** Young children can practice tossing a beanbag over a line or into a big square

✳ **NOTE:** For the perfect hopscotch stone, see page 27

Let's Play

For Most Kinds of Hopscotch

The setup: For any game of HOPSCOTCH, the diagram is drawn on the sidewalk with chalk or scratched into the dirt with a stick. The spaces must be big enough for everyone's feet to fit when hopping, without touching the lines.

The play: Decide if you are playing with stones or just hopping as in ESCARGOT (page 29); whether stones are to be tossed and picked up, or whether you are going to kick them back to the baseline; and whether you're hopping on an assigned foot, picking your own best foot, or going twice around with different feet.

Rules/scoring: The usual rules for being out are similar no matter which design you use. You're out if: you or the stone lands on a line; you step in an initialed square; you drop the stone; you or the stone lands out-of-bounds. Changing from one foot to another or putting two feet down is a miss, too, unless the diagram you are using (such as POTSY, page 27) allows it.

Finding the perfect stone: Whether you call it a stone, a marker, a potsy, or a puck, finding the perfect one is the key to the game, in my opinion. You want it to be flat and thin so that it will sit where it lands, rather than bouncing or rolling out-of-bounds. But you don't want it so thin that it will break when it lands, so beware of shale or mica. Once you find the perfect hopscotch stone, which can be hard to find, save it for future games, because good stones are easy to find, but perfect ones … now, they are a different story!

The toss: The toss for HOPSCOTCH is very much like the one used for skipping stones on a pond. Hold your stone as shown. Bend your wrist, as if you are about to toss a Frisbee. Then snap your wrist and let the stone go, aiming it so that the flattest side will stay parallel to the ground. And just as when tossing a ball or Frisbee, keep your eye on the target, not the stone.

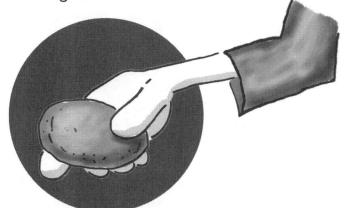

With your hand parallel to your body, elbow bent slightly upward, hold the stone between your pointer finger and thumb. Curl your other fingers slightly underneath so the stone rests on them for balance.

POTSY
(A.K.A. NEW YORK HOPSCOTCH)

To land in Squares 1 and 2, Squares 4 and 5, or Squares 7 and 8 when a stone is not in either of the two squares, land on two feet at the same time, one foot in one square and one foot in the other. To turn at Squares 7 and 8, land with both feet. Then, jump and turn at the same time, landing on both feet simultaneously, but facing the other way (toward the baseline). Continue back.

The setup/play:

1. Using the NEW YORK HOPSCOTCH design (page 27), each player takes turns and plays through until he is out.

2. On your turn, toss your stone onto Square 1. Hop on one foot into Square 2 (you never hop into the square that holds your stone) and continue hopping to Squares 7 and 8. Then, turn (see caption, page 27), and hop back, picking up your stone that is in Square 1, while balancing on one foot in Square 2 (you always pick up your stone from the square *before* your stone's square). Hop to the baseline.

Rules/scoring:

✳ Keep playing until you either miss or have completed the whole course, picking up your stone from all eight squares. If you don't make it around the full course eight times, leave your stone in the last completed square, and pick up where you left off on your next turn.

✳ If someone's stone hits yours and knocks it out-of-bounds or onto a line, you must begin at Square 1 again. If someone's stone knocks yours into another square, you play from that square on your next turn.

✳ If you complete the whole course (eight times around), you may "call" any square number and toss your stone. If it lands in the square you called, you may put your initials in that square. After that, no one except you may land there. Either way, it is the next person's turn.

To win: When you stop playing or there is no place to hop because of initialed squares, the player with the most initialed squares wins. Or, if you play that everyone can put his initials in any square — even if someone has already initialed it — then to win you need to be the first player to have her initials in every square. (That is the way we usually play.)

Everyone loves HOPSCOTCH. Here Lady Liberty is playing NEW YORK HOPSCOTCH.

Variations:

KICK THE POTSY: Toss your stone in Square 1 first (Square 2 on next turn, etc.). Kick your stone around the course, using the same hopping foot to kick, and landing in each square along the way, without the stone or you landing on a line or out-of-bounds. No limit on kicks. Continue tossing, hopping, and kicking. (Use the POTSY design, page 27)

8-SQUARE: Using the 8-SQUARE design (same as BOXBALL, page 23), you play up to Square 4 and then come back by way of Squares 5 through 8. Turn on one foot only. Best when played with KICK THE POTSY rules.

ESCARGOT: A favorite in France [*escargot* (es-car-GO) means "snail" in French], in this HOPSCOTCH version no stone is used in the hopping part of your turn. Hop on one foot all the way to the rest space at the center of the snail (home), then hop back on the same foot. If you complete the course successfully, you toss your stone into a square, and if it lands within bounds, write your initials on that square. From then on you are the only one who can step on that square. The same game can be played on the **JAPANESE LADDER** course. There are two ways to play:

✳ Each player takes just one hopping turn at a time, or

✳ Each takes a second round on the other foot per turn.

To make it harder, number all the squares. Before tossing the stone, you must call out a number. If your stone lands in that square, write your initials. If not, no square for you. Play until all the squares are marked with initials or no one can make a hop.

ENGLISH HOPSCOTCH: Play on the 8-SQUARE design (page 23), but instead of hopping on one foot, you hold the stone between your feet and hop from square to square. If you drop the stone or land on a line, your turn ends.

To win any of these variations: The first player to get through the whole course (that is eight times around in KICK THE POTSY, NEW YORK, 8-SQUARE, and ENGLISH), or, if using initials, the player with the most initialed squares at the end of the game.

ESCARGOT

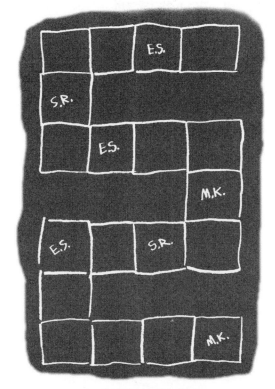

JAPANESE LADDER

MARBLES

Now, we're not talking about world championship marbles here. No sirree, sir! We're talking crouching-in-the-dirt-with-your-friends marbles, which to my way of thinking, is much more fun. At least the way we play, it is!

* **PLAYERS:** Any number, but 2 to 6 are ideal
* **AGES:** 8 and up
* **SITE:** Outdoors (on dirt) is best
* **MATERIALS:** At least 6 marbles, plus 1 shooter per player. Usually each player has several marbles (they should be easily identifiable so they don't get mixed up).
* **GOAL:** To capture as many marbles as you can
* **TYKES:** Not appropriate. *Please keep track of the marbles, and put them all away when you are done playing.* Children under 3 years old can choke on them. Thank you.

Let's Play

The setup/play: Draw a circle in the dirt about 6 feet (2 m) in diameter. Each player's marbles are put randomly in the center. Each player takes a turn trying to shoot the others' marbles out of the circle, using (duh!) the shooter marble.

Rules/scoring:

* The shooter marble must remain inside the circle for the shot to count. As long as you hit a marble, you get to shoot again, from wherever the shooter stopped inside the circle.

* Once your shooter goes outside the circle, or you miss a hit, your turn is over. If your shooter is still inside the circle, it stays there until your next turn.

To win: The player with the most marbles at the end wins!

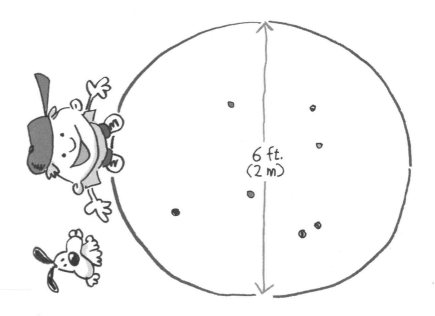

6 ft. (2 m)

Great Games!

Variation: Make a shallow hole in the center of the playing area. Each player contributes a marble, scattering them around the playing area. Use the shooters to try to knock the other marbles into the hole. Any marble you knock into the hole, you get to keep, and you get to shoot again.

Just a Few of Us!

Rain or Shine, These Games Are Fine!

So, my best buddy drops by the house at 4:00 on a Saturday afternoon. We both had had a lot of chores to do, because there were tons of leaves to rake, being that it was late October. And we had done a lot of homework on Friday night. (It is our opinion that about the first of October, school takes on a much more serious tone, and teachers definitely load on the work.) It was turning cooler out-doors, getting darker earlier, and we were kind of tuckered out and feeling a little sorry for ourselves. Oh, woe is me! Then, my sister Debby appeared with some cookies she had baked. We got some cider and, hmm, things didn't seem so bad after all. Nothing that a couple of good games wouldn't cure.

Sam says: **"I could have invented that!"** Have you ever sat around after playing some game that you bought in a store and said that? I mean, what is so special about the Parker Brothers or Milton Bradley, or even Edward Lowe? Edward, uh, who? Edward Lowe — who not only invented BINGO, but also brought the game YAHTZEE to the market (and maybe to your house).

Here's the story: Supposedly, a Canadian couple played a game they made up on their yacht. Their friends enjoyed playing it so much that in 1956 they asked Edward Lowe, who they knew was a game inventor, to produce their game so they could give it to their friends as gifts. Lowe also thought it was a great game, so he bought the rights to manufacture it and changed the name from YACHT to YAHTZEE, adding a few variations.

And that's the story, folks! So maybe there's a game invention in your future, perhaps one that you play on the porch. You could call it PORCH, or bet-ter yet, PORCHEZEE!

Great Games!

YACHT

You can't control the roll of the dice, but you can develop some good strategies for this game. We always play very competitively, which makes it even more fun. So jump into the spirit of the game and see if you think Edward Lowe knew what people like in their games!

Let's Play

The setup: Make a scorecard before the game begins, copying the sample shown here, putting each player's name across the top. The numbers shown in brackets are the best possible scores you can get for each category listed down the left side of the page (see YACHT scoring, page 34). For the ones through sixes, you need to get three dice of the number you are rolling or else you score zero.

* **PLAYERS:** Any number, even I (play against yourself for best score!)

* **AGES:** 8 and up

* **SITE:** Good everywhere, lots of fun on long trips

* **MATERIALS:** 5 dice and a dice cup; pencil and paper

* **GOAL:** To get the maximum score in each category, so that you can get the highest total score of all

* **TYKES:** Not appropriate. *Please keep track of the dice, and put them all away when you are done playing. Children under 3 years old can choke on them. Thank you.*

YACHT Best Possible Score	Janet	Megan	Chad
1s [5]			
2s [10]			
3s [15]			
4s [20]			
5s [25]			
6s [30]			
Little Straight [15]			
Big Straight [20]			
Full House [28]			
Four of a Kind [30]			
Chance [30]			
Yacht [50]			
Total [278]			

This is YACHT (not YACHTZEE) scoring.

Just a Few of us!

········ Yacht Scoring ········

Little straight: 1-2-3-4-5 You must have all dice to score 15 points, or else you score 0

Big straight: 2-3-4-5-6 You must have all dice to score 20 points, or else you score 0

Full house: Three of any one number and two of any other number (so, 3-3-3 and 5-5 scores 19 points)

Four of a kind: Four of any one number plus the odd number!

Chance: Best score you can get out of your three tosses (put aside highest number each toss)

Yacht: Five of any one number for 50 points

Have a YACHT **party,** where small groups of about three to four players each play a round. Everyone writes down her score and then the groups shuffle. (We play that you pick out of a hat for each round, and all who get papers marked with red play together, all green together, all blue together, and so on). When the evening is over, add up your scores. The highest total is the winner. I'm not a game player usually, but this is really fun and a lot of laughs. We play adults and kids all mixed together.

— Mitch

The play:

1. To choose who goes first, roll one die. We play that the lowest count goes first, and the play continues clockwise.

2. For your turn, you get three rolls of the dice, putting aside the dice you want to count after each roll, and then rolling what is left for your remaining rolls. There are two ways to play:

✴ **Roll of the dice:** You must fill whatever is next on your scorecard, with the highest score you can get. For the first turn, that is *ones,* and on the next turn, you roll for *twos,* and so on. This is more a game of chance with less strategy involved.

✴ **Strategies:** You decide which category you want to shoot for *(full house, straights, sixes)* on each turn, putting aside any dice that help you reach that goal in your three rolls per turn. You may change your mind about what you are shooting for during your turn (maybe a *full house* was your original goal, but it looks like the best you can do is two *fours).* You must fill in something on the scorecard (even if a zero), and you can't change it once it is entered at the end of your turn.

Rules/scoring:

✳ At the end of your turn, no matter which way you play, you have to assign a score to each line on the scorecard — there are no passes. For some scores, you may have to enter zero.

✳ Keep the scorecard handy, so that before each turn the player can see what he needs to fill in. Remember your goal is to fill in every spot with as close to the highest possible number as you can.

To win: Add all of the points at the end of the game. The person with the highest score wins.

Variations:

✳ For the first few rounds while you are learning, just play to get as many *ones* on the first roll, *twos* on the second, and so on in order through *sixes*.

✳ Play several games and have the winner be the highest total scorer for all rounds.

✳ Let a *little straight* be any four dice in sequence, rather than five, and allow a *big straight* to be high (2-3-4-5-6) or low (1-2-3-4-5).

KiDS SPEAK!

Playing strategies: Once you play a few times, you'll begin to find strategies that work best in different situations. I always go for the higher-scoring (and more difficult) categories first, such as the *straights* or a high *four of a kind*. That way, if the rolls go well, you can be sure you have those high points taken care of early on. If you don't get the rolls you want, just fill in the *ones* or *twos* with as many as you have (or even zero). Later, you can try to make up any missing amounts by rolling four (instead of just three) *threes*, *fours*, *fives*, or *sixes*. It's a good strategy that works for me, so try it!

— Emily

These games are fun to play anywhere, anytime. They're especially good when you have to wait a long time or when you are traveling, but we like to play them in the sand at the beach, too. Need two players, ages 8 and up.

Dots & Lines

Play in the car, an airplane, anytime! With two players and a pencil and paper, you are good to go.

The play: Draw a grid of 100 dots, 10 rows down and 10 rows across, spacing the dots as evenly as you can (graph paper helps a lot). Take turns drawing a line to connect two side-by-side dots. You may connect them horizontally or vertically, but not diagonally. No other dots may be inside the lines.

If you make the last line to form a square using four dots, put your initials inside the box, and take another turn. Play until no more lines can be drawn. The player with most initialed boxes wins. Try playing with triangles, rectangles, and other shapes, too.

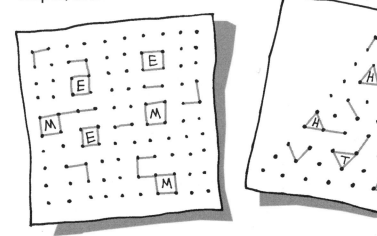

Four-Field Kono

In this game, you capture the other player's pieces by substituting your playing piece for hers. It's not as easy as you might think! All you need are two players, paper, pencils, and eight pieces each that look different from your opponent's (use white buttons/black buttons, pennies/nickels, Cheerios/Froot Loops).

The setup: Draw a grid with four lines across and four lines up and down. Using all playing pieces, set one piece on each intersecting line, so that your two rows face your opponent's two rows. There are no empty spaces.

The play: The first player jumps over one of her own pieces and lands on, or captures, the other player's piece, removing it from the board. Then the other player takes a turn.

Rules/scoring: All moves and captures must go along the lines; there are no diagonal moves. Players must capture whenever possible, but if not possible, the player must move one space along the lines.

To win: The game is over when all of one player's pieces are captured. When no moves are possible, the player who has captured the most pieces wins.

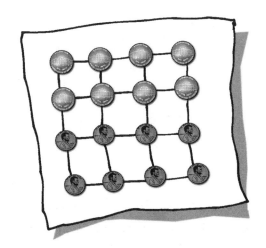

●SALVO

Do the moves and strategies for this game sound familiar? They will if you play the Milton Bradley game BATTLESHIP. This is a good game of strategy to play anywhere — even via e-mail with a pen pal or friend.

* **PLAYERS:** 2
* **AGES:** 8 and up
* **SITE:** Anywhere
* **MATERIALS:** Paper and pencils

BRITNEY

Each player draws TWO grids of 100 squares, 10 rows down and 10 rows across, on two pieces of paper (graph paper works great). Label one with your name and one with your opponent's name. Mark the squares with letters and numbers as shown.

Let's Play

The setup: On your own grid, shade in a fleet of 4 ships: a 5-square battleship, a 3-square cruiser, and two 2-square destroyers. The ships can be drawn horizontally or vertically, but not diagonally, and the squares can't touch each other, even at the corners. Sit so neither player can see the other player's shaded grid.

The play:

1. Each turn consists of firing seven shots (or *salvos*) from your fleet. Call out the names of the shots, such as B2, E6, F8, F7, D1, and so on, marking the squares you call on your opponent's grid. Use a number 1, so you'll know these were your first shots. Repeat for every turn.

2. The other player marks the salvos on his grid, too, and then reports any damage, like this: *Three hits; two on the battleship and one on a destroyer.* But he doesn't tell *which* squares were hits!

Rules/scoring: A ship sinks when all the ship's squares have been hit. The player reports the coordinates of the sunken ship, and thereafter takes fewer shots on his turn: a sunken battleship equals three fewer shots; a cruiser, two; and a destroyer, one.

To win: The game ends when a player's last ship sinks. The other player is the winner.

Variations: To make it more like BATTLESHIP, fire only one shot per turn, and respond with *Hit, Miss,* or *Sunk.* Also, you can use five ships: a carrier (5 spaces), a battleship (4 spaces), a cruiser (3 spaces), a submarine (2 spaces), and a destroyer (2 spaces).

Just a Few of Us!

PICK-UP-STICKS

PICK-UP-STICKS takes the same kind of hand agility that JACKS (pages 41 to 43) does, although PICK-UP-STICKS is definitely a little easier — especially if you stay focused. For one thing, with PICK-UP-STICKS you can use two hands! The trick is to use the black stick to help you lift something, for example, at the tip, without moving any others. You can also use it to flip a stick away from the others. The more you play, the more tricks you learn.

* **PLAYERS:** 1 to 4
* **AGES:** 7 and up
* **SITE:** Indoors, on a smooth surface
* **MATERIALS:** One set of 41 pick-up-sticks including one black one
* **GOAL:** To pick up as many sticks from the pile as possible without moving any other sticks
* **TYKES:** Kids ages 5 to 7 may begin to learn this game by playing on a carpet, where the sticks won't roll or move as easily

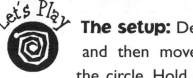

Let's Play

The setup: Decide who goes first, and then move clockwise around the circle. Hold all the sticks in one hand, stand them on end pointing straight up, and quickly let go. The sticks should fall in a ring, but sometimes they tumble onto each other, which makes play more difficult.

The play: Players take turns trying to pick up the sticks, one by one, without moving any other stick. If you remove a stick successfully, place it next to you and continue on until you cause one of the other sticks to move. Even the slightest wiggle of a stick means it's the next player's turn.

Rules/scoring:

* Any stick that is moved or dropped is left where it falls.
* *The black stick:* Some play that the first player to pick up the black stick may use it to help pick up his other sticks. Others play that the black stick is not included in the original setup, and anyone may use it when he wants.

To win: Play continues until the last stick is picked up. The player with the most sticks wins. Or, assign varying points for the different stick colors, making some sticks more valuable than others. The player with the most points wins.

DOMINOES

This particular game is called DRAW DOMINOES, but there are many, many more versions, some easier and some much more complex. All the bones are mixed by placing them facedown on the playing surface and moving the dominoes around with the palm of your hand.

* **PLAYERS:** 2 to 4
* **AGES:** 8 and up
* **SITE:** You need a flat surface, like a table or floor
* **MATERIALS:** One set of dominoes (28 pieces, called *bones*)
* **GOAL:** To be the first to get rid of all of your bones or to reach an agreed-upon number of points

Let's Play

The setup: Each player draws bones — seven each for two players, five each for three or four players — placing theirs on their long edges, hiding them from the other players' view. The rest of the bones are left facedown, in the bone yard.

Sam says: OK, I just can't tell you a lie. I mean, after all, we are becoming friends here, with all of us sharing our favorite games and strategies. So, anyway, here's the truth: I never played DOMINOES before I began writing this book. Oh sure, I've stood them up on end and made as long a trail as I could and then I touched one and bingo-bongo, all the others toppled just as smoothly as could be. But to play a game of DOMINOES? Just never seemed to happen. The reason I finally learned was because my good buddy Mikey drew the cover for this book and, well, take a look: The whole border is made of dominoes! So, I figured there's only one thing to do, and I did it. I finally learned the game. I'm still sort of new at it and I can't give you any tips, but I do see how it grows on you. I asked my friend Emily to explain it to you, as she's a longtime player and she's the one teaching me. She likes playing games as much as I do, and she is great at coming up with strategies (*and* her own rules)!

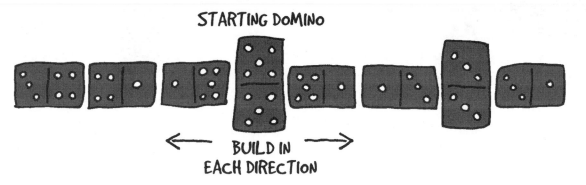

STARTING DOMINO

← BUILD IN →
EACH DIRECTION

The play:

1. To set the highest domino, the player with the highest *doublet* (a domino with the same number of dots on both ends) goes first, putting her double faceup on the playing surface. The player to her left goes next, setting a bone that has a matching number of dots on an end perpendicular to the doublet, on the middle line.

2. The play continues from there, with each player adding a bone that has a matching set of dots on at least one end. No bones are added to the ends of the doublets, just from the two sides that are played. Any additional doublets are placed in the same way as the first one, crosswise to the other bones.

BONES?

Rules/scoring:

✴ If you cannot make a match, you draw a bone from the boneyard until you find one. If all the bones are used up, you pass on your turn.

✴ When a player has no bones left, he says, *Dominoes!* The other players must show their dominoes, adding up the total of all the dots showing on their unplayed bones. The total of all the players' unplayed bones is the winner's score! Thus, the strategy throughout the game is to get rid of your high numbers, so you won't give a high score to your opponent should he "go Domino" (play his last bone).

To win: The first player to call *Dominoes!* wins the game. Usually several games are played, and the overall winner is the first person to reach some agreed-upon number, such as 50 or 100.

If no one wins the game, yet all players must pass, the player with the fewest dots on her remaining dominoes wins that round. To determine her score, she subtracts the number of dots she has left from the total of the other players' remaining dots (so she is docked for the dominoes she couldn't play).

Great Games!

JACKS

This is the game to play if you have nimble fingers. I always move something (I'm better at other kinds of games), but I still like JACKS because my sisters get so into it and are so competitive about it. Susan once won the county JACKS championship! You should have seen her after that: Jane had to bring her back to reality by winning when they got to the (impossible) *Around-the-world* Fancy (page 42).

Now, if you don't have the foggiest idea what I am jabbering about, listen up, because I have to admit it, JACKS — even for clumsy people like me — is a great game!

* **PLAYERS:** 1 to 3 or so

* **AGES:** About 7 and up

* **SITE:** Indoors or out, on a smooth surface like pavement, a floor, or even on a big old table (with permission because you might scratch it)

* **MATERIALS:** 10 jacks (pronged playing pieces) and a very small ball that has a good bounce to it. If you don't have jacks, use smooth, small pebbles. (You can buy an inexpensive set of jacks with a ball at toy stores.)

* **GOAL:** To advance through the predetermined number of Fancies

* **TYKES:** Not appropriate. *Please keep track of the jacks, and put them all away when you are done playing.* Children under 3 years old can choke on them. Thank you.

* **NOTE:** For Fancies, see page 42

Let's Play

The play:

1. First person up holds all the jacks in her hand and then drops them all at once. For *onesies,* she then tosses the ball gently in the air with her right (or dominant) hand, picks up one jack with the same hand, and then catches the ball with the same hand after one bounce. She does that for all 10 jacks, setting each one aside each time.

2. When *onesies* is complete, she then drops the jacks again, and does *twosies,* repeating the same process, only this time picking up two jacks at a time. And so on, all the way through *tensies.* If the number does not divide up evenly, pick up as many of the full number as you can, and then the remaining jacks (as in *foursies,* pick up four, four again, and then two).

TWOSIES!

Just a Few of us!

Rules/scoring:

✳ A miss is any time you don't pick up the correct number of jacks, you miss catching the ball, you use both hands, or you move a jack that you are not picking up. If you miss, the ball and the jacks go to the next player. On your next turn, you continue where you left off, but with a new toss of the jacks.

✳ Fancies (right) are a big part of this game. Either predetermine the order of Fancies or let the player who is ahead select a Fancy, which everyone else will follow. Each Fancy starts at *onesies* and goes through to *tensies*, too, only each step follows the Fancy's style.

To win: To be furthest ahead when you stop playing; or, to have completed all of the agreed-upon Fancies first; or, to be furthest ahead when the agreed-upon playing time is up.

✳ ✳ ✳

CHICKEN IN THE COOP

·············· Fancies ··············

Once you've gone through the *onesies* to *tensies*, you start Fancies, which is when the real fun begins! You say: *First* (or second, third, etc.) *Fancy, follow my Fancy, I choose Sweepsies* (name of Fancy)!
Here we go:

✳ *Knuckles:* Pick up the jack and then tap your knuckles on the surface before catching the ball.

✳ *Knock, knock:* Just like *knuckles* except you knock on the surface two times.

✳ *Chicken in the coop:* Cup your left (or nondominant) hand, leaning it with the pinkie side against the playing surface. Each time you toss the ball, instead of picking up the jacks, sweep them into your cupped "chicken coop" all the way through *tensies*.

✳ *Around-the-world:* Toss the ball, pick up the jacks, and while holding them, move your hand around the ball in the air, before it hits the playing surface. Catch it after the bounce.

✳ *No bouncies:* Toss the ball, pick up the jacks, and catch the ball before it bounces.

✳ *Sweepsies:* This is a two-part Fancy. Toss the ball and move the correct number of jacks, as if you are sweeping, and catch the ball. Toss the ball again and this time pick up the jacks.

Sam's Sisters' Strategies for Jacks

✳ The higher you hold the jacks in the air, the more spread out they will fall. So, for lower numbers such as *onesies* and *twosies*, you'll want to hold them higher, so you won't accidentally touch another one. But for higher numbers, you'll want to release them closer to the playing surface, so they *will* stay closer together and it will be easier to pick up more of them with one swoop of your hand.

✳ The higher you toss the ball, the more time you have to pick up the jacks and then catch it. But, the higher you toss the ball, the less control you have over where it will land, making the ball more difficult to catch.

✳ For the lower numbers, actually pick up the jacks with your fingers. For the higher numbers, sort of capture the jacks as you sweep your hand on the playing surface, only closing your hand on the ones you need.

✳ Have a plan before you toss the ball. If you know where you are going to grab the first four jacks, on, say, *foursies*, you are more likely to get them all.

✳ It is actually possible to pick one jack off the top of another without having them both move, but you need to study how they are balanced before tossing your ball up in the air.

✳ Take it from us, and don't play on rough pavement or on floors with splinters!

✳ People with large hands always blame their errors on the size of their hands. People with small hands always blame their errors on the size of their hands. Hmm! What do you think about that?

CHECKERS

Lots of people play CHECKERS, but we like to play with tough rules: Once you touch a piece you have to play it, and if you can't, you miss your turn. If you have a lot of people at your house, it is fun to have CHECKERS tournaments with play-offs. (Just remember to ask your friends to bring their checkerboards.)

* **PLAYERS:** 2
* **AGES:** 7 and up
* **SITE:** Anywhere with a flat surface
* **MATERIALS:** A checkerboard and 24 checkers (12 of each color)
* **GOAL:** To capture all of the other player's pieces

Let's play!

Let's Play

The setup: Place the checkerboard with the light-colored corner on the right side of each player. Line the checkers up on opposite sides of the board, in rows, placing the checkers only on the dark squares of the board (the light squares are not played).

The play: Players move one piece per turn, diagonally forward. You move only one square at a time, unless you are able to make a jump by jumping over your opponent's piece to the next space, which must be empty. (Think of it as leapfrogging, only you are using checkers to go over your opponent.)

 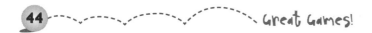 Great Games!

Rules/scoring:

✳ Black always goes first.

✳ Whatever piece you touch first is the one you must move. If that piece is not playable, you miss your turn. Your turn is over when you take your hand off that piece — no second guesses or retakes! (Told you we play a tough game!)

✳ You cannot jump over your own checkers.

✳ Your jumping checker must be diagonally next to the checker you are jumping.

✳ The jumped checker is captured by the jumper, who removes it.

✳ You can jump more than one checker in a single turn as long as you land in an empty black square before jumping forward again with the same checker.

Double Jump

✳ Any piece that makes it to the farthest row on the other side (called the *king's row*) is immediately crowned with one of the pieces your opponent captured. You say, *King me,* and the opponent makes you a double-decker player. What's so great about being *kinged?* The king can move backward and forward, jumping in any direction.

To win: The first player to capture all of her opponent's pieces (or if the other player can't move) wins.

What About Chess?

If you notice, many of these games involve strategy. And that is why people love them so much. CHESS is the ultimate game of strategy. And you'll notice that CHESS players are kind of fanatics about the game: They play and play and play. And when they are not playing, they often are watching other people play. So, I didn't include it in here because it would have taken every page of this book! Really! People have written hundreds and hundreds of pages about how to play CHESS.

Here's what I suggest you do to learn or improve your CHESS game: Join a CHESS club. Lots of places have beginning CHESS groups. They even play against teams from other schools. Is there one at your school? If not, ask a teacher to help you organize one. Or, ask at your library, the "Y," the Boys and Girls Clubs, Scouts, religious teen groups, and recreation centers sponsored by your town or city. And don't be shy about being a beginner: CHESS players seem to really enjoy teaching new players!

P.S. All of the above could be said about the very popular card game called BRIDGE, too!

The Gang's All Here!

What do you do when the gang's all here? Well, if you want to have a superior, most awesome time, you know the answer, so let's hear it now!

The games here are mostly tried-and-true favorites that have been played in the far corners of the world. (I know, the earth is round so there are no corners. You are all just too smart — or smart-alecky! — for me!) Just ask some adults you know! I bet that they played some of these. Either way, ask them to join in because fun is the name of these games.

So, is everyone here and ready to play? Take a gander at what's in store for you here! Let the great games begin!

Sam says... Looking for more games for a big group? See Play Ball! (pages 84 to 105) and Gotcha! Tag Games! (pages 77 to 83). Also see the index under Number of Players and Sites. When choosing teams, look over some fair play suggestions on pages 8 to 9.

LEMONADE
(A.K.A. TRADES* OR NEW YORK)

When you were a little kid did you play the variation of this game called WHEN I GROW UP, I WANT TO BE …? I did and I loved it! If you've never played LEMONADE before, I'd say it is sort of a combination of RED LIGHT, GREEN LIGHT and CHARADES.

* **PLAYERS:** Most fun with a crowd

* **AGES:** 8 and up

* **SITE:** Best played outdoors, but can also be played in a gym

* **GOAL:** To avoid being tagged by the other team, while getting the most players on your team

* **TYKES:** See WHEN I GROW UP, I WANT TO BE … (page 48)

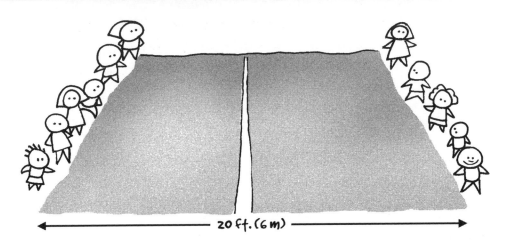

⟵ 20 ft. (6 m) ⟶

Players divide into two teams and stand on parallel baselines about 20 feet (6 m) apart. A centerline is marked, 10 feet (3 m) in from the baselines.

Let's Play

The setup/play:

1. One team (Team 1) secretly decides on a trade that they will all act out, or *pantomime*.

2. Both teams advance to the centerline, saying as they go:

> **Team 1:** *Here we come!*
>
> **Team 2:** *Where from?*
>
> **Team 1:** *New York.*
>
> **Team 2:** *What's your trade?*
>
> **Team 1:** *Lemonade.*
>
> **Team 2:** *Give us some!*
>
> **Team 1:** *If you can … P.B.* (The initials are the first letters of the trade, such as P.B. for "playing ball," or D.R. for "driving a rig.")

3. Team 1 acts out the trade, without talking. As soon as Team 2 guesses the trade correctly, they shout the trade name out and then chase Team 1 players back to their baseline, tagging as many as possible.

*In this game, a "trade" is a kind of job, such as a house painter, tennis player, or violinist.

Rules/scoring:

✳ Players who are tagged join the other team and then they (Team 2) decide on a trade, and the game is repeated.

✳ If one team doesn't guess the trade correctly and gives up, the other team chooses one member of the opposing team to be on their side. Then they take another turn with a new trade.

To win: The game continues until both teams have taken an agreed-upon number of turns, or until one team has all the players! The team with the most players at the end wins.

When I Grow Up, I Want to Be ...
When kids ages 4 through 7 want to play together, they can play a variation of TRADES (page 47). They take turns acting out different jobs that they would like to have, and everyone guesses.

Quick Takes

KIDS SPEAK!

I like TRADES because of the guessing part, but some of my friends like the running part best. This game isn't much fun if all the good runners are on one team or all the good guessers are on a team. When the teams are divided evenly, then everyone has a much better time.

— Vicky

 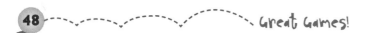

CAPTURE THE FLAG

Here's a game that is hard to stop playing — even when it gets dark. That's when people get out their flashlights! Really! We aren't the only ones who enjoy CAPTURE THE FLAG, though, as it goes way back to the time of knights and castles in the Middle Ages. It just proves that a really great game can be around for a long, long time — as in hundreds and hundreds of years!

* **PLAYERS:** Best played with 10 or more, enough for 2 equal teams

* **AGES:** In mixed-age groups, give each team an equal mix of players

* **SITE:** In a field or large yard

* **MATERIALS:** 2 pieces of material to serve as "flags"

* **GOAL:** To get the other team's flag, carry it back to your home base, and avoid having your flag or teammates captured!

Let's Play

The setup:

1. Make a dividing line in the middle of the playing area to determine the two sides. Each team has a jail and home base near its back line.

2. Divide players into two teams (page 16). To tell the teams apart, have one team wear caps, bandannas, or a piece of fabric around each player's upper arm.

The play: Each team has an agreed-upon time, such as five minutes, to hide its flag, usually somewhere near its "jail." After hiding the flag, players try to cross over to the other team's side to search for its flag and capture it.

Rules/scoring:

✻ If you are tagged when you are on the opponent's side of the field, you must go to its jail. Captured players can be freed *only* if tagged by a member of their team.

✻ If you capture the other team's flag and are tagged on your side, you have to drop the flag where you are tagged.

To win: The first team to capture the other team's flag and bring it back to its home wins. Or, you can play that the game is over only when one team has both flags.

Variations:

✻ A great variation: Tagged players still go into the other team's jail, but the newest tagged player keeps only one foot in jail and forms a line with other tagged players (in the order that they were captured) out toward their home base. If a free teammate tags a prisoner, then all of them are free, and they can go back to home base without being tagged.

✻ Tag with water balloons or snowballs! Each team gets an equal number of filled balloons or soft snowballs, depending on the time of year. These props can be used to "tag" players. Best played in bathing suits or with mittens, and tons of fun and laughs.

✻ Eliminate the jail so that anybody tagged becomes part of the other team.

Quick Takes

Stealing Sticks

Place piles of four or five sticks toward the center back of the two areas, and mark a "prison" on each side. Similar to CAPTURE THE FLAG, the object is to capture the opponent's sticks without being caught. A player can be freed from prison if one of his teammates touches his hand. The team that has all its sticks and players free wins.

HURRY!

JAIL

HIDE & SEEK

It's hard to say what part of this game is more fun — the hiding or the chase! This game probably brings the best memories of living in my neighborhood in Tarrytown, New York, where I grew up. We played for hours on summer evenings. Everyone was welcome. No one complained of our boisterous screeches as we yelled, *Ollie, Ollie in free!* when we reached home base without being tagged.

* **PLAYERS:** About 6 to 10 are best

* **AGES:** Good for mixed ages

* **SITE:** Outdoors in a big yard or park with lots of bushes and trees; in a basement (with permission)

* **MATERIALS:** Bug spray if you are playing on a summer's evening

* **NOTE:** Playing at dusk is a lot of fun, (1) if you have permission, (2) if there are no cars around, and (3) if you are in a safe place with some streetlights or outdoor lights.

Let's Play

The setup: Players agree on a home base and the limits of the hiding area before beginning. Players pick one person to be the Seeker; the rest are the Hiders.

The play: The Seeker shuts his eyes and counts from one to 50. When done, he calls, *Ready or not, here I come!* And the game begins. The Seeker looks for the Hiders, while the Hiders try to remain hidden until they have a good opportunity to quickly and quietly run to home base without being tagged.

Ready or not, here I come!

SPOT

Rules/scoring:

✳ Any Hider who is discovered must get to the base before the Seeker, without being tagged. If the Hider reaches home first, he yells, *Home free!* If the Seeker reaches it first, the Hider is out.

✳ Players can race for home at any time — they don't have to be found. If they get there untagged, they yell, *Ollie, Ollie in free!*

✳ Any players still in hiding at the end of the game are called in by the call, *Ollie, Ollie out are now in free!*

To win: The last person found or the first person in to home base without being tagged wins. The winner can choose to be the Seeker; otherwise, the first person tagged is the next Seeker.

Sam says... **Always Fun & Always Safe!** Everyone wants the perfect hiding place, but please DON'T be tempted to hide in unsafe places. NO HIDING EVER anywhere in or near a car, an old trunk or refrigerator, a stuffy closet or attic, a space that is really too small for you, caves, deep holes, or sand or gravel pits. Stay where you can peek out at the other players, and where there is plenty of fresh air to breathe and space to stretch! And when the game is over, make sure everyone is accounted for, OK?

SARDINES

This reverse HIDE & SEEK is — no kidding! — *packed* full of fun. *Yukka, Yukka, Yukka!*

> ✳ For the general game information, please see HIDE & SEEK, page 51.

ERK! someone needs a bath!

Barney

The setup/play: All the players choose the Sardine and agree on the limits of the hiding area. Then, the players all hide their eyes (no peeking!) and count out loud together to 50, while the Sardine hides. At number 50, everyone begins to look for the Sardine.

Rules/scoring: If you spot the Sardine, don't tell anyone. When no one is looking, slip in and hide *with* the Sardine. Eventually everyone starts to disappear until the last person finds the whole group, packed in together — *just like sardines!*

To win: The first one to find the Sardine gets to hide as the Sardine in the next round, if he chooses to. If not, then the last one to find the Sardine hides on the next round.

Sam says... It takes all kinds of people to have a great game, and in SARDINES, where the players get really close — maybe closer than you'd like — you need to be tactful, but firm. If someone sitting on your foot is too heavy, or someone is breathing his bad breath right in your face, or is just too close for you to feel comfortable in any way, simply say, "My foot (or arm, or shoulder) is going to sleep. Could you move a little so I can get comfortable? Thanks." That's all there is to it, and no one has hurt feelings or is embarrassed, but you are out of a situation that wasn't comfortable for you. Good going!

KICK THE CAN

The pace of this game is much faster than it sounds here. People should be running to home base, changing places, and evading the Seeker at every opportunity. We like to play in the dark with just the lights from the street lamps and houses, or using flashlights.

✳ See the Game Box for HIDE & SEEK, page 51. Here the goals are slightly different, as you'll see, and you'll need a can, block of wood, stick, stone, or puck.

Let's Play

The setup: One player is chosen to be the Seeker, and all other players are Hiders. A home base is selected. To begin, Hiders distract the Seeker from protecting the can so that one player can kick the can as far away from home base as possible. As soon as the kick is made, all Hiders run and hide, leaving the Seeker alone.

POW!

I HATE being the can!

Rules/scoring:

✳ The Seeker must kick the can back to base — no hands allowed — and then look for the other players.

✳ If the Seeker spots a hidden player, the Seeker runs back home, puts her foot on the can, and calls, *I spy (person's name)* or *One-two-three on (person's name)*, taking the Hider prisoner. Meanwhile, if the Hider realizes he has been seen, he tries to run to home base, get there first, and kick the can far away again. The Hider and any prisoners can hide again if the Hider reaches home first.

✳ The Seeker may leave the can untended while searching for Hiders, but she risks having someone run to the can and kick it. If that happens, the Seeker kicks the can back to the base, while all prisoners scatter and hide again. If the Seeker tags the kicker before he reaches the can, then the kicker is captured.

✳ While the Seeker looks for Hiders, Hiders can sneak home and kick the can, thereby freeing all prisoners.

✳ The Hiders change hiding places frequently — you are not allowed to stay long in one spot. Any prisoner can look for remaining Hiders and wave them in when it's safe, freeing all prisoners.

To win: The game is over when everyone is captured, or everyone is tired and needs a break! The first one captured is the next Seeker.

KIDS SPEAK!

I had the best time when my Uncle Mitch and Uncle Bruce both joined a big group of us kids for a great game of KICK THE CAN! I'll never forget how fast they ran to kick that can before one uncle could tag the other one out. They looked like they were flying and they were laughing so hard at the same time! I thought for sure they would collide!

— Zachary

STATUES

Here's a game that everyone can play, no matter how old. It's sure to turn any glum chums into gigglers! Very young kids should play FREEZE DANCE. (You don't want your little cousin or neighbor turning into a whirling top now, do you?)

* **PLAYERS:** Older kids will want at least 8
* **AGES:** All ages
* **SITE:** Anywhere
* **STRATEGY:** Concentrate on someone other than "It"
* **TYKES:** 4 players; play FREEZE DANCE version (page 57)

Let's Play

The setup:

1. The person who is "It" swings each player, one at a time, by the arms in a circle, and then releases her. Some versions let the players choose how fast they want to be swung: easy, medium, or really fast. "It" may ask, *Coffee, tea, or milk?* A reply of *Milk* means easy, *Tea* is a slightly faster spin, and *Coffee* is as fast as "It" can possibly spin you!

2. The swung player spins around and must hold whatever position (right down to the expression on her face) she is in when she stops.

3. "It" then moves on to the next player, until all the players are in statue positions. Now "It" goes from statue to statue, trying to make the statues laugh, move, or otherwise break position, following the rules.

Oops!

Rules/scoring: Players decide ahead of time what "It" can do to make the statues move or change expression. Is joking, being silly, or making funny faces and movements what is permitted, or can "It" tickle with a blade of grass, too? If a statue moves but "It" doesn't see the movement, the statue is still in the game.

To win: The last statue becomes "It" in the next round.

Variation: FREEZE DANCE is the same game except it is played to music instead of having "It" spin the players. All players dance to some music, while "It" has his back to the group. "It" stops the music and whirls around. All dancers must hold their poses, while "It" tries to get them to move, as in STATUES.

So here's the story on tickling: Don't! That may seem harsh, but many people have a real problem with tickling. To them, being tickled feels as painful as being hurt or slapped. To others, tickling is a violation of their personal space. If you don't mind being tickled, then go ahead, and let people you know tickle you. But never assume someone is OK with tickling. Got it? Good!

Big Group, Little Space

Sometimes, either by chance or by inviting people, you end up with a lot of people at your house. Here are some games that don't need a lot of space and can be played indoors or out. Girls and boys are equally good, as are people with varying abilities, and that makes it all the more fun. Sure it will get noisy, but that's just a sign that everyone is involved and having a super time together. So, rock on!

SPOONS

This game is one of my favorites, played whenever there are lots of people in very silly moods.

PLAYERS: 5 to 10 work best

AGES: Mixed ages from 7

SITE: Wherever the players can sit about equidistant to the center

MATERIALS: A deck of cards and spoons for all but one player

The setup: All players are seated in a circle or where they can reach the spoons that are set up in the center of the playing area. Spoons alternate direction between handle and bowl.

The play: One player begins moving cards around the circle clockwise. Each player must pick up the card, glance at it, and place it facedown in front of his neighbor, keeping the cards moving at a fast pace without gathering in front of any player. Without disturbing the group, the player who gets the joker reaches in and grabs a spoon. That is the signal for other players to grab a spoon quickly and quietly, until all spoons are gone. The player without a spoon gets an S for S-P-O-O-N. The player with the joker is the next dealer; spoons are reset, and play repeats.

To win: The last player to get SPOON spelled out or the person with the least letters when the game stops wins.

WINK

(A.K.A. ASSASSIN)

Don't be put off by the "also known as" gruesome name … this is great fun! It's really best played when you're playing *another* game at the same time (CLUE would be a perfect companion!), or just hanging out with friends playing cards or listening to music. Depending on the craftiness of the players, the game can go on all evening!

* **PLAYERS:** Especially fun with large groups
* **AGES:** 8 and up
* **SITE:** Anywhere
* **MATERIALS:** Paper, pencil, and bowl
* **GOAL:** To identify the "murderer" before you are "killed," or, if "It," to "murder" everyone before they find you out

Aack!

The setup: Put folded slips of paper — one for each player — in a bowl, with one paper marked with an X. Each player picks a paper and whoever gets the X is "It."

Rules/scoring:

* "It" starts by gradually winking at one player, very subtlely, without letting on to the other "victims." Then wink again … and again …

* If you are winked at, you wait a minute or two, and then casually say, *Dead!* (with lots of "dying" antics, of course!). The "waiting part" is very important, or it is easy to spot the Assassin. Once you are "dead," you are out of the game.

* The remaining "live" players try to figure out who the Assassin is, keeping watch on all the other players. The Assassin should pretend he doesn't know who it is either. If you think you know who the Assassin is, you can make a guess, but if you guess wrong, you are "dead" too.

* When the Assassin is found out, write down the number of victims. Then everyone picks a paper from the bowl again, and the game starts over with a new Assassin.

To win: The Assassin who "murders" the most victims by the end of the evening wins.

CATEGORIES

This rhythm game is great fun to play with groups as large as 20 people. Everyone can enjoy it because no matter how clever you are, how good a listener you are, or how great your sense of rhythm is, you may end up the first out or the winner. Just begin by having a good time and don't worry about when you miss, because one thing is for sure, you are going to miss — a lot of times!

* **PLAYERS:** Most fun with a crowd

* **AGES:** 8 and up

* **SITE:** Anywhere everyone can sit in a circle and see each other

Let's Play

The setup:

1. All sit in a circle with legs crossed. Choose someone to be the first leader. That player starts the rhythm as shown below.

2. The syllables of the words follow the rhythm as shown (page 61).

Tap both knees twice.

Clap both hands twice.

Snap fingers one hand at a time.

The play:

1. All players continue the rhythm, with the leader beginning by doing the finger snaps, and naming something in her category of ice creams:

Choc (snap on one hand) *-olate* (snap other hand)

2. The next player has to say a new flavor on the snaps: tap, tap; clap, clap; snap, snap; and on snap, snap, the next player might say, *Va-nilla!*

3. Continue around the circle with all players keeping the rhythm but the next one naming something in the category. You're out of the circle if you can't think of something in the category in time, you repeat something that has already been said, or you hesitate and miss the snap, snap.

To win: Play continues until only one person is left. That player starts the next category.

CATE - GORIES
(tap knees)   (tap knees again)

SUCH - AS
(clap once)   (clap again)

ICE - CREAMS
(snap one   (snap other
hand's fingers)   fingers)

CHARADES!

CHARADES is lots of fun — probably because anyone can guess anything. Silly, serious, impossible, or easy, somehow this game always results in lots of laughs.

* **PLAYERS:** Good with at least 5 players on each team, or with fewer, play 1 against all

* **AGES:** 8 and up

* **SITE:** Indoors or out

* **MATERIALS:** Paper, pencil, bowl, and timer or watch

* **GOAL:** To act out a phrase or word so your teammates guess it as quickly as possible

Let's Play

The setup:

1. Establish teams if you have enough players so one team member acts and her teammates guess. Or, play that one person acts and all others guess.

2. Write sayings or quotes; book, movie, or song titles; or persons, places, or things on slips of paper with your name and put them in a bowl.

3. To start, one player chooses a prepared slip of paper, and gives approved signals (see page 64) about the topic on the paper. Players take turns acting out the topic, for her team or all players. The actor's goal is for others to guess as quickly as possible. (No guessing if you wrote it!)

JAWS?

STAR WARS?

BAMBI?

The play:

1. As the actor, you can use gestures to *mime* (act without words) each word, or the syllables in the words.

2. The play of the charade follows a certain order.

* First, use motions to "tell" the audience what topic the word or phrase belongs to (page 64).

* Next, tell how many total words by holding up the appropriate number of fingers, and then which word you are going to start with (first, second, third, etc.). You can act out any word in any order.

* Finally, indicate how many syllables the word has (page 64) and which syllable you are acting out first.

3. The other players call out guesses. If a guess is correct, you can point to the person who said it, nod your head, or put your finger on your nose (a signal that means "You got it!"). Then move on to next word or syllable, holding up fingers to specify what you are acting.

Rules/scoring: No talking allowed, or mouthing the words, or pointing to the real thing.

To win: The person who guesses the phrase correctly does the next charade, either for her team on the next turn, or for all players immediately. The person or team with the greatest number of correct guesses at the end of the agreed-upon time wins.

Picture Charades

Good at guessing and drawing stick figures? That's all you need to know to play this guessing game, which is very similar to CHARADES. Here instead of acting out your topic so your team can guess, you sketch it out. If you've played the store-bought game PICTIONARY, well, this is very much like that, only free!

Charade Acting Signs

Even though there is no talking on the actor's part in CHARADES, there are plenty of gestures that are part of the game, and they are almost as good as speaking.

✳ **To show the kind of topic:**

   Book title: Open your hands, palms up

   Song: Pull a pretend "string" of musical notes from your mouth

   Movie: Pretend you're running a movie camera

   TV show: Draw a box around your head and shoulders

   A saying or quote: Make quotation marks in the air

✳ **To show that you are acting out syllables:** Hold out your arm and pretend to chop it; then hold up fingers to show which syllable

✳ **Gestures to "explain" what you are doing:**

   Pulling on your ear means the word you need to guess "sounds like" whatever you act out next (They say *ocean;* sounds like point to self, *me.* Answer = *sea.*)

   Pulling your hands apart means "say the same word but in a longer form" (*sing … singer*)

   The T-shaped time-out signal means "the"

   Almost pinching your thumb and first finger together means small word, such *as a, an, is,* and *it*

✳ **To encourage a player who is on the right track,** beckon him with your two hands, meaning make more similar guesses

BOOK TITLE

SONG

MOVIE

TV SHOW

Great Games!

phun with werds

Get it? You know, "phun" sounds like the word fun. Now do you get it? Ah, fun with words! So, you say, what's so great about that? Well, it did trip you up, even if for just a minute, right? And that's part of what word games are about. They stop you in your tracks, like meaningless gibberish at first, get you frustrated, and then, bingo bango, a broad smile covers your face with that "aha" look. Word games are about lots of laughs (and sometimes groans). You'll find, once you get into the mind-set of a game, that you know a lot more than you ever believed, and you may discover a clever hidden sense of humor that you never knew you had.

Sew, lettuce knot waist any moore thyme, four wee don't no wear thistle lead two.

Sam says: For more games that are perfect for two to four players, please see Just a Few of Us!, pages 17 to 45, and the index under Number of Players.

POULTRY IN MOTION

Sam says... I already know what's going through some of those noggins out there. "I'm no good at this stuff." "This is supposed to be fun?" "This Sam person has lost it now!" Well, let me just say this about that: Word games have very little to do with any of "that stuff." They are more about being able to see familiar things in a different way. If you are good at building things, knowing whether something will fit in a tight space if you turn it a little this way or that, listening to the words people say rather than jumping to conclusions, thinking imaginatively, and, most of all, you have a very good sense of humor — well, that is the "stuff" of word games. And, a word game is only as good as the person who howls with laughter at your funny jokes and puns. So, please, cool your heels for a moment and see how it goes.

BELOW C LEVEL

FORTUNATELY/ UNFORTUNATELY

Are you an optimist (a "this is great!" person) or a pessimist (an "uh-oh, I think we've got a problem" person)? Try this game to see just how positive or negative — and outrageous — you can be!

KIDS SPEAK!

This is fun when we are all in silly moods and everyone tries to top the previous person in how preposterous the situation becomes. If you play this realistically, it is more challenging to think of things to say, but it isn't nearly as much fun. The thing is, we kids like to say outlandish things and use made-up language. This game is a perfect place to do it!

— Sarah W. and (the other) Sara W.

Let's Play

The play: Begin telling a story by saying one sentence. It can be about anything, as long as you can use the word *fortunately* in your sentence: *Fortunately, we have plenty of food for the trip.* The next player continues the story, using the word *unfortunately* in a way that relates to what was just said. *Unfortunately, it got sopping wet in the storm.* The next player continues the story, back on the positive side. *Fortunately, there is a store just ahead.* Then the pessimist: *Unfortunately, all the stores are closed today because all the electricity is out.* The story continues, always keeping close to the story line and relating to what was just said.

Rules: You can either play that you make the story utterly ridiculous or that what you say has to be somewhat possible (which makes it much more difficult).

To win: No winners but you are out if you can't think of anything to add.

HINK-PINK

Do you remember my mentioning my buddy Mikey, who designed the book cover (page 29)? Well, if you look on the book cover again, you'll see why we are playing HINK-PINK now. You got it! Mikey put HINK-PINK right there for all the world to see. You see Mikey is not only a great illustrator (he drew all of the illustrations in this book!) but he is a word guy from the get-go. He plays with words the way most of us play with a plate of pickled beets and liver — shuffling them around all over the place. And I've got to tell you, if you want to laugh, play word games with my good buddy in his new book, *Wacky Word Games.*

So here we go — HINK-PINK, HINKY-PINKY, and HINKIDDY-PINKIDDY all the way home!

HINKY-PINKY this, INFATUATED FELINE.

Smitten kitten?

PURRR...

TUNA

Let's Play

The play: There are strict rules when playing the "official" HINK-PINK, but this is your buddy Sam talking, and I have to say it is way, WAY, WAY more fun to play the "unofficial" game. (It taxes your brain less, but still gives it a good workout!) So, unofficially speaking, what you do for HINK-PINK is give a two-word clue to which all other players respond with an answer that fits these parameters:

✳ a two-word response that means the same as the clue

✳ both words in your response have the same number of syllables

✳ both words in your response rhyme

One player might say *rodent dwelling* and another player responds *mouse house* (rodent = mouse, dwelling = house). The two-word response has the same meaning as the clue, the same number of syllables (one per word), and rhymes (mouse and house). Taking it from the top one more time, one player might say *comic rabbit* and another might respond *funny bunny.* Get it? Good. You can play this with two or more players, anyone can guess, and if no one guesses, the same person gives a new clue. So have fun hinking-pinking for hours in the car, standing in line, or swinging in the hammock with your friends — feet dragging on the ground, looking up at the sky.

To win: No score, no winners — fun for all!

GHOST

This game is fun
anytime, anywhere,
day or **night**,
rain or **SHINE**,
winter or summer,
spring or fall,
good mood or **bad**,
happy or sad,
noisy or **quiet**,
WITH YOUR BUDDIES or the 'rents,
sick or well,
serious or silly,
on earth or in space,
windy or calm,
LIGHT or **DARK**...
well, you get the idea.

B

B-O

B-O-O

B-O-O-K

RATS!

The play: The first person begins by saying a letter — *F*, for example. You say another letter that would allow a word to be spelled but wouldn't finish the word. So, you might say *E* (because lots of words begin *FE*), but you couldn't say *P*, because there's no word that begins *FP*. Another person adds another letter, say, *B*. Play continues until you can't add any more letters.

Rules: If you add a letter and it spells a whole word, you get a G, then an H, and so on. Once your letters spell G-H-O-S-T, you're out of the game.

You can challenge, if a player adds a letter and you think there's no word that can be made (see *FP* above). If it's true that there is no such word, that person gets one of the G-H-O-S-T letters. But beware! If you're wrong, *you* get the letter! Whoever gets a "ghost" letter begins the next word.

To win: Last one to have GHOST is the winner!

●AUNTIE SUE IS STRANGE
(A.K.A. GRANDMA IS STRANGE)

To tell you the truth, I always had a problem with this game — not because it wasn't fun, but because of its name, GRANDMA IS STRANGE. I always felt as if I were insulting my grandma or someone else's grandma. But the game is fun, so, now I am thinking, let's just all agree to change the name of the game. How about AUNTIE SUE IS STRANGE? (Of course, if you have an Auntie Sue, you might want to change it to AUNTIE LETITIA IS STRANGE unless of course, you have an Aunt Letitia …)

SHE LOVES DOCTORS, BUT HATES DENTISTS!

DUH!

Let's Play

The setup: Think of a secret peculiarity of an imaginary Auntie Sue. She might love words with double letters, or things that are only one color, or things that happen just once a year — you name it.

The play: You might say, *Auntie Sue is so strange. She loves dogs, but hates cats.* (Here, Auntie only likes words with Os in them, but don't tell anyone.) If another player thinks he's guessed the peculiarity, he tests out his idea with a question: *Does your Auntie Sue love opera and hate rap?* Your answer (in this case) is *yes*, because opera has an O, but rap doesn't. If yes, that player gets to either guess again (to confirm he is on the right track), or he may guess Auntie's secret peculiarity. If he's wrong, the game continues, with the leader giving more clues; if he's correct, he becomes the next to think of another peculiarity of Auntie Sue.

Variation: If the player realizes he's guessed Auntie's strange secret, he, too, joins in giving the other players clues. *She loves carrots and corn, but hates pickles and peas.*

WORD SQUARES

This game is tantalizing, because no one knows what the other person is doing or even where he himself is going. It is sort of like playing a combination of SCRABBLE and BINGO while blindfolded. Along the way you'll learn some good strategies, but sometimes, even those let you down.

Your basic Word Squares setup

The setup: All players need paper and pencils to draw a large square and divide it into 25 small squares, making your own grid, sort of like a crossword puzzle.

The play:

1. Each player calls out one letter at a time, and all players place it on their grid, wherever they want (that's part of the strategy — deciding where to place the letters, because you don't know what letter is coming next).

2. Continue calling out letters (you can repeat letters as often as you want and you don't need to use all letters), until all the squares are filled.

Rules/scoring: Each person circles the words they have made:

✳ Words must have at least three letters.

✳ Words can go horizontally, vertically, or diagonally. Some players allow backward words, too — decide what your "house rules" are before you begin.

✳ Words within words count, too, so *car* and *card* in the word *cards* would equal three words.

✳ Assign a point for each letter of each completed word, or decide that 5-letter words get, say, 10 points, 4-letter words, 5 points, and 3-letter words, 3 points.

To win: The person with the highest score wins.

Variations: If you want to keep everyone on their toes, after you add up your scores, switch papers. If someone else or the whole group can find a word on yours that you missed, they get two points per letter.

PAPER SCRABBLE: Make a larger grid (nine squares by nine squares, or 10 lines across and up and down) and play like SCRABBLE. The first person writes a word, and the next person adds a word, using at least one letter from the previous word. Each letter in a word is worth one point. The person with the highest score at the end wins.

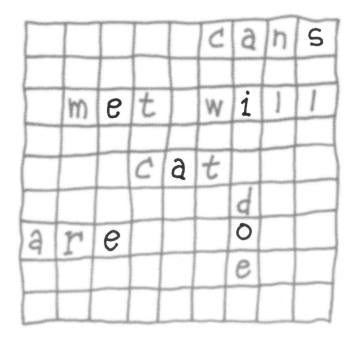

Your basic word Squares setup with optimal vowel placement

VOWELS RULE!

KiDS SPEAK!

Here's the only thing you need to know to be really good at WORD SQUARES: Vowels rule! I always put an A in the center and I place other vowels three squares in (on the diagonal) from the corners. If I get more vowels, I put them three squares out (vertically and horizontally) from the center A. Second best hint: S is the most valuable non-vowel letter with runner-ups T, R, and M. Place them where they can begin a five-letter word or, in the case of S, where it can end just about any word to give you two words in one.

— Jane

Quick Takes

Twenty Questions
(a.k.a. Animal, Vegetable, Mineral)

You can play this as a group all guessing together, which is my favorite way, or you can play it as two teams, or you can play it one on one. One person thinks of a common object (let's say *milk*) and announces to everyone what category — animal, vegetable, or mineral — the object falls under. (Milk is animal.) The other players try to discover what the secret object is by asking questions that can be answered with either *yes* or *no*. You are allowed only 20 questions total, so you want to ask questions that will eliminate larger possibilities, rather than just eliminating that specific question. Someone might ask, *Is this something people eat? Yes.* Someone else might ask, *Is this something that you have to chew? No.* and so on.

If, after 20 questions, no one has guessed the answer, the person tells the group and then tries to stump everyone again. If the group guesses, the person who made the correct guess is the one to think of something next.

Crambo (a.k.a. I'm Thinking of a Word …) is a rhyming game, with the goal of guessing the mystery word. The fun part is that the rhyming and guessing go both ways.

"It" thinks of two words that rhyme. The first word is the mystery word (say, *call*), and the second is the clue (*tall,* for example). "It" says, *I'm thinking of a word that rhymes with tall.* The other players try to guess what the mystery word is by asking questions with *descriptions* of words that rhyme with the clue. *Is it a narrow passageway in a building?* "It" would say, *No, it isn't a hall.*

The first person to guess the mystery word wins. But if "It" can't guess what it is the other player is describing (such as *mall* for a place that you can shop), that player wins and gets to think of the next mystery word.

License Plates

There are several ways to play this game but these are the two that I like best:

Read me! In this game you try to decipher the message on vanity license plates (the ones that you pay extra to have your own name or a message on). So, can you read these?

Occupations: Think of a job. Use letters and numbers to create a license plate that would be appropriate for a person with that job. Can you guess the occupation of the person with the license plate **DIGITUP**? What about **ILUV2S8**?

answers: archaeologist, hockey player

Draw the head, neck, body, one arm, other arm, one leg, and other leg. At that point the person is hanged.

Hangman

All you need are paper and a pencil, and a good word or two. Then guess away, before you are — yikes — hanged!

The Hangman (the person thinking up a word) represents all the letters of the mystery word with blank lines. He also draws a gallows. The other player (or players) guesses a letter that might be in the word. If correct, the Hangman puts it in all places in the word; if not, the letter is written down, and the Hangman draws a head hanging from the gallows. If you repeat a letter by mistake, the Hangman must draw part of the person. The player continues guessing, letter by letter, trying to figure out the word before a whole body is drawn.

BALDERDASH

This game is similar to a board game with the same name that is lots of fun to play. In both versions, be prepared to howl with laughter (*balderdash* means nonsense). You won't believe how clever and funny some of these definitions can be!

FLAUTIST; A person who makes jewelry from earwax...

Let's Play

The setup: You'll need a dictionary, and several pencils and pieces of paper. "It" finds a word in the dictionary that she suspects no one will know. She reads the word out loud and writes down the real definition. The other players each write down a definition. Each player's goal is to make up a definition that others will believe is correct. "It" collects all the definitions, mixing in the real one. "It" reads all the definitions in a very natural voice.

The play: The other players close their eyes as "It" reads the definitions a second time, voting (by raising their hands) for the one they think is correct. The players get one point for each vote for their "incorrect" definition. If no one guesses the correct one, "It" gets three points. If a player guesses the correct definition, that person gets two points.

Variation: In **DICTIONARY,** the goal is to write down the correct definition of the word that "It" says. If nobody defines the word correctly, the person who found the word gets a point. If a player does write the correct definition, that person gets a point. The person with the most points after several rounds wins.

WORD CHAINS

"Set the rules" before you begin because there are many different ways to play this game. If you pick a general category, such as food, the game can go on for a long time. If you prefer a real challenge, pick something more difficult, such as kinds of trees or flowers.

Spaniel!

Labrador!

Rottweiler!

Russian Hound!

Dachshund!

Dalmation!

Norwegian Elkhound!

Dingo!

Let's Play

The play: Basically, you select a category (food, animals, countries, cities, sports, movie stars, or whatever) and then the players name words in that category. The trick (there is always a trick to a good game!) is that the word you name must *start* with the *last letter in the previous player's word*.

So, if the category is food and the person before you said, *soup,* you could say **p**eas, and the next person could say **s**alad.

Rules: If you use a name like New York, it is the first letter of the first word (**N**) and the last letter of the last word (**K**) that you use for the word chain. The same is true of names of people, unless you are playing last names only.

If you can't think of anything that hasn't been said before when it's your turn, or if you make something up and someone else successfully challenges you, you get a letter in C-H-A-I-N against you.

To win: The player with the least letters or the last one still in wins.

Variations:

✳ In **ALPHABET WORD CHAINS**, you name words in the chosen category by alphabetical order rather than by the last letter. So, for cities, players might say in turn, **A**lbuquerque, **B**oston, **C**hicago, etc.

✳ In **I PACKED MY GRANDMOTHER'S SUITCASE,** you also name words in alphabetical order. So you would say, *I packed my grandmother's suitcase and in it I put* **a**pples, **b**rownies, **c**oats, **d**olls ....To make it more difficult, you can set some limitations in size (can't pack a refrigerator, for example), or in categories. To make it even more difficult, each player must rename what has been said before, beginning at A, and then add their new word.

¡Gotcha! Tag Games! ¡

With a name like Taggar, you might assume that TAG is a favorite game of mine, and you'd be absolutely right about that! I mean, what's not to like? It's fast, it's fun, everyone can play no matter how big the group, and there are so many variations on the theme that there is always bound to be a new variety to play — just to keep things interesting! So, what's your pleasure? SHADOW TAG, ELBOW TAG, FLASHLIGHT TAG? Decide quickly, because ... you're "It"!

sam says: For choosing "It" or teams, please see pages 12 to 16. If you are looking for greater variety in games with a group of people, see The Gang's All Here!, pages 46 to 64 and Play Ball!, pages 84 to 105, or see the index under Number of Players.

✳ TAG BASICS ✳

✳ **PLAYERS:** Any number, about 8 to 20 are best

✳ **AGES:** Any and all ages, but be careful of the littler ones

✳ **SITE:** A grassy area outdoors is best, but a gym or large basement can work. And don't forget the snow and the beach!

✳ **MATERIALS:** None, except for a few specific games

✳ **TYKES:** Little ones love this, but play with them separately so they don't get hurt

For Most Tag Games

The setup: When it comes to TAG, most everyone shouts, *Not It!* so the choosing of "It" can become rather troublesome. Have no fear, because you know what is near — right? All those fun and silly ways to choose "It" and solve the problem of "Not It" (pages 12 to 15).

Rules/scoring:

✳ The player who is "It" closes her eyes and counts to an agreed-upon number like 25 while everyone else scatters. Then "It" pursues the others, until she tags some-one. The tagged person then becomes "It" or, if players agree, joins the original "It" in chasing down every one else. Each ver-sion has different twists on how you're tagged or become "It."

✳ Some TAG versions have a safety or home base, where players can go for a quick rest. Players agree ahead of time how many times you can touch safety, and how long you can stay there.

✳ TAG can get a little rough if instead of a gentle tag, it turns into an all-out body tackle. Easy does it, good buddies, OK?

KIDS SPEAK!

We usually play that we can take a break by yelling *"Times!"* But there is someone who seems to yell *"Times!"* just as he is about to be tagged. That way he never becomes *"It."* So, some of the kids want to play "no timesies," which I think is really hard. Now he is never *"It"* and I'm always *"It"* because I get tired of running. I finally got everyone to agree to two *"Times!"* a game. I think that is fair to everyone. Besides it is fun to be *"It"* a few times — just not all the time.

— Jean

DUHHH... TAG!

ELBOW TAG

You need to have a good sense of cooperation to make this game work.

Let's Play

The play: If you have an odd number of players, play so that one person is "It," and everyone else hooks arms at the elbow with a partner. The partners try to avoid hooking arms with "It." If "It" hooks arms, the player's partner must become the new "It."

With an even number of players, one player is "It" and another is the Runner. All the other players hook arms with a partner, and scatter. The Runner tries to hook the elbow of any player, setting that player's partner free to now become the new Runner. If "It" tags the Runner before she hooks onto another person, the Runner becomes "It." Then "It" can run and hook on to someone else.

Variation: DRAGON TAG is a variation of this game, requiring a larger number of players. Four people are "It," linking arms to make the dragon. Staying linked, they chase the others and capture one of them by forming a circle around him. Then the tagged player joins the dragon. Play continues until all the players are part of the dragon.

FLASHLIGHT TAG

Play in a safe outdoor area and ask permission before using the neighbors' backyards. If you go to a park, then you will need some adults with you, OK? No playing where you have to cross roads.

Sam says:

Night games seem to be memory-makers. Is FLASHLIGHT TAG your favorite tag game? It's mine, right up there with nighttime HIDE & SEEK and nighttime KICK THE CAN! Sometime when you're not playing and are just sitting around, get a few people talking about their favorite nighttime game memories. Get some of the older folks in on the talking, too, and I guarantee people will have the most amusing stories to tell, some accompanied by great gales of laughter and others with a bit of a tear in an eye as they recall times gone by. We used to play FLASHLIGHT TAG at night after a fresh snowfall, when our homework was done. We were slipping and sliding so fast and falling so often that we never even noticed that it was bitter cold outside. What's your favorite nighttime game memory-maker?

Let's Play

The play: "It," armed with a flashlight, searches for the other players and tries to tag one of them with the flashlight beam. When another player is beam-tagged, she becomes the new "It." A safety such as a tree or bench is designated somewhere in the play area where you can't be tagged. Usually you can only use the safety twice per game.

TAG! You're it. And stay away from my soda!

DRAGON'S TAIL

Here is one of those games where you have to know how to cooperate — or else! It is really hard if you are playing with a group of people who don't know each other very well, because then everyone is equal, without familiar roles such as leader or follower.

Each team needs a scarf, sock, or piece of fabric for a tail.

The setup: Divide into teams of four or five players (you can have several teams). Each group lines up in single file, with each player holding onto the shoulders of the player in front of her. The player at the front of each line is the head of the Dragon, and the last player in each line, with a scarf or sock in her back pocket or waistband, is the tail.

Rules/scoring: At a signal, the player who is the head tries to get the tail of another Dragon. Meanwhile, the tail is trying to stay away from any other heads. The middle players have to hang on so the body doesn't break. If a Dragon's body breaks at any time or its tail is stolen, that team is out.

To win: The last Dragon with the most captured tails wins.

Variation: TEAM DRAGON'S TAIL is played with all members on one team. At "go," the player at the head tries to catch the tail (the last person in the line). If the head successfully catches the tail, he or she continues to be the head (leading the group). If the body breaks, the head becomes the tail, and the next in line gets to be the head.

FOX & GEESE
(A.K.A. PIE)

Here's another favorite game that we always played in the snow, when it got so slippery that chasing and tagging could become almost impossible. Lots of fun anywhere else that is good for TAG, too. Usually about six players work best, rather than the bigger groups used for many TAG games.

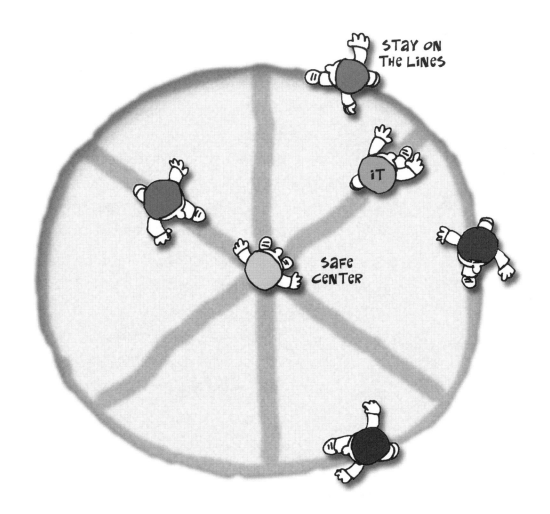

STAY ON THE LINES

iT

SAFE CENTER

Let's Play

The setup: Stamp out a circle in the snow or sand (or draw one) large enough to run around easily. Divide it into six segments with paths that meet in the middle, like pie wedges or the spokes of a wheel. The player who is "It" is the Fox; all the others are Geese.

Rules/scoring: "It," or the Fox, chases after the Geese, who are safe only when standing on the center spot. When running you must stay on the paths: No jumping across to another path or stepping out with one foot when rounding a corner. As Geese are caught, they join the Fox in chasing the other players.

To win: The game continues until all the Geese are caught; then, the first Goose caught becomes the new Fox. So, run, run, run for your lives!

Variation: To make the game more challenging, make a maze of trails, some leading to the center and some to dead ends, rather than just having spokes.

Touch Tag

Nothing could be simpler or more straightforward than this original. When "It" tags another player, that person becomes "It." No one is out and there is no safety.

Variation: In TOUCH ONE, TOUCH ALL, each person tagged joins "It" in chasing down the others. The first person tagged is "It" in the next round.

Shadow Tag

This is a good game to play in the late afternoon. "It" tags another player by stepping on her shadow, then she becomes "It."

Play it in bright moonlight, too!

Hospital Tag

This version of TAG is the funniest of all. When "It" tags someone, that person becomes "It," but with an injury: The new "It" must run holding one hand on the place where he was tagged, or "injured."

Freeze Tag

Another one of my top Taggar Tags! When "It" tags a player, that person must immediately freeze in place and position (even your face). Then, while "It" is chasing someone else, another player can sneak up and melt the frozen player, who can then run again in the game. But, if "It" sees the frozen person move, that person becomes "It." Or, if "It" catches the "melter," then that player is "It." If you're frozen three times, you're out.

Ball Tag

You'll need a playground ball or a beach ball for this free-for-all game. (Did you ever notice how often a ball manages to find its way into games?) "It" tosses the ball gently, trying to hit one of the players. The player who is hit becomes "It." No one hit? "It" tries again, or you can play that a player grabs the ball and tries to hit "It." If the player succeeds, "It" is out of the game.

Play Ball!

If you can amuse yourself for quite some time by tossing a ball against a wall or walking while bouncing it (and not stepping on any sidewalk cracks, of course), then this is the game section for you. I know that I'd be hard pressed to sit idly by when there was a ball in my presence. I mean that ball is just aching for me to pick it up and toss it. And who am I to disappoint a perfectly good ball?

Now, we're not talking about pro ball here — no baseball, softball, soccer, basketball, tennis, or ping pong — because you can find lots of people to teach you who know those challenging games far better than I do. No, I'm talking about playing ball games that require lots of ingenuity, some skill if you want to get really good, and are just plain fun.

So, as I said to start out, "Play ball!"

BALL? THIS iS a QUASi-FUNCTiONAL, PLiaBLe aND PSEUDO-SYNTHETIC GAMING ORB!

Sam says: For choosing "It" or teams, please go to pages 12 to 15. To see a listing of all ball games in this book, go to the index and look under Ball Games. If you are looking for other games for groups, see the index under Number of Players.

············· Keep It Safe! ·············

Let's be serious for just one minute, OK? People tend to get very involved when playing ball — running, cheering, scrambling, and generally not looking where they are going. And that is fine as long as you are in a safe place.

Don't ever play ball in the road or near a road.

When you are playing hard, chances are that no matter how careful you usually are, you won't stop to look both ways before dashing into the street. Too many serious accidents have happened just like that. So keep it safe, play on a ballfield, in a park, or in a yard where cars aren't a factor. Thanks, all you great ball players!

Two Great Balls for All of These Games!

Different games are best played with a few basic kinds of balls. They cost very little and as with just about everything you do, using the right "tools" makes everything easier. If you don't have any kinds of game balls at home, save your allowance to buy these two kinds, because they are the bargain of a lifetime: They cost very little and give you hours and hours and hours of good times.

✳ **A Pinky Ball:** This ball (about the size of a tennis ball) is the basis of most Wall Ball, Stoopball, Slapball, and O'Leary Bouncing Ball games. The original kind is hollow and can bounce very high (its nickname is "High-Bouncer"), yet it is soft enough so it doesn't hurt your hand when slapping or punching it. Some similar-sized balls are good, too, except they may be solid rubber and harder on your hands. A tennis ball is a good substitute for a Pinky.

✳ **A Playground Ball:** This large, soft, rubber ball, about 10" to 12" (25 to 30 cm) in diameter, is perfect for all the games where you throw the ball at someone as in Kickball, Spud, and Dodge Ball because it doesn't hurt when you are tagged with it. Some people call them gym balls, because they are perfect for playing indoor ball games, too. Be sure to buy hollow balls with thick rubber. A beach ball is a fair substitute in some games.

I'm glad my name isn't Pinky.

FOUR SQUARE

My guess is that this has been a favorite game of schoolkids since before there was television, which means a long, long time ago! Just about all of the ball players I know love this game. The key to success is paying attention and opening your hand wide to slap the ball. Be sure to use your full arm to swing.

* **PLAYERS:** 4 or more

* **AGES:** 8 and up

* **SITE:** Outdoor paved area or indoors in a basement or gym

* **MATERIALS:** White chalk, Pinky or tennis ball

* **GOAL:** To slap the ball into another player's square in such a way that he is unable to slap it to the next player's square; to stay in Square 4 the longest

* **NOTE:** See Sam Says ... on page 95 for how to slap the ball

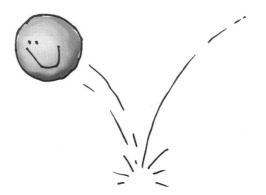

The setup: Draw a large square, about 8 feet (2.5 m) on each side; then draw two lines to divide it into four squares. Number the squares 1 through 4 as shown, with Square 1 having the lowest rank and Square 4, sometimes called the King, having the highest rank.

The play: Use a choosing method (pages 12 to 15) to decide who gets which square. To start, Square 4 serves the ball by bouncing it once in his square and then hitting it toward one of the other squares, using just one hand. The receiving player lets the ball bounce once and then hits the ball to any other player.

Rules/scoring: The play continues until one of the following misses occurs:

✳ You hit the ball before it bounces once in your square

✳ The ball bounces twice in your square

✳ You hit the ball out of bounds

✳ You use two hands to hit the ball

If you miss, you move to the lowest-ranking square, and the other players then move up one rank to fill the vacancies. If there are more players than squares, you go to the back of the line, and the person at the front of the line gets to move onto the lowest square and play. Whoever is in Square 4 serves the ball to start the play again.

To win: The player in Square 4 for the longest time wins.

Variations:

KING CALLS: Square 4, or the King, can change the bouncing rules, usually at the beginning of a round. In KING CALLS NOW, the bouncing rules can be changed at any time — even with the ball in midair! So the King might say *bounce tinies* or *bounce and spin.* Here are some more bounce calls:

> *Quick change:* Call the direction of the ball in the square, such as clockwise or counterclockwise.

> *Tinies and High-bouncers:* The bouncer has to hit a very low bounce or a very high bounce.

> *Bounce, then Stumpers:* Bounce, and then do any of the Stumpers, pages 19 to 20.

SIDEWALK TENNIS: Instead of four squares, there is a single line between two squares. Players slap the ball after one bounce back and forth over a line, like playing tennis without a net.

SPUD

Why is this game so much fun? Everyone gets involved in the action and it is not competitive, but rather, it is shared fun with a group of buddies or people you just met. SPUD is one of those games that people love no matter where they grew up or where they live now. It goes quickly and keeps you on your toes. There are a lot of games that are sort of like SPUD, but as far as I know, this is the "real" version.

* **PLAYERS:** Best with a group of up to about 10
* **AGES:** Anyone
* **SITE:** Outdoors, in a yard or park; or in a gym
* **MATERIALS:** Playground or gym ball
* **GOAL:** To avoid earning all the letters in the word SPUD
* **TYKES:** Play by just calling out a name and rolling the ball to her. Then she calls a name and rolls it to someone else.

Let's Play

Rules/scoring:

* Choose a person to be "It," and gather in a circle around "It."

* "It" tosses the ball in the air, while calling out a player's name. The named player runs to catch the ball while all the other players scatter as far and as quickly as possible. When the ball is caught, the Catcher shouts *Spud!* and all the players, including the Catcher, must freeze.

* The Catcher *gently* throws the ball at any player. That player tries to catch the ball, or she moves her body, using one foot as a pivot (she cannot move both feet), to avoid the ball. If the targeted player is hit, she gets an "S," but if the Thrower misses the targeted player or the targeted player catches the ball, the Thrower gets the "S."

* The player with the "S" tosses the ball for the second round of play. The game continues as players with S-P-U-D are out and only one person is left.

To win: The last person still in wins.

Variations:

* Some people play that the Catcher can take four giant steps toward a player, before throwing the ball to tag her.

* "It" counts to 10 out loud. As he counts, the rest of the players scatter. When he reaches 10, they all freeze.

* Players count off by numbers and are called by their numbers instead of their names. This works best if a lot of players don't know each other, or if there are a couple of players who "hog" the ball, calling each other's names over and over.

* To make the game last longer, spell a longer word, such as "asparagus."

* **CALL BALL:** This is very similar to SPUD except the ball is not thrown at anyone, which makes some players more comfortable with CALL BALL than with SPUD. Here, all players have a number. "It" tosses the ball up in the air and calls out a number. The called person has to run into the center and try to catch the ball before it bounces. If a catch is made, the Catcher is "It"; otherwise, the would-be Catcher is out and "It" tosses the ball up again. The last player still in the game is the winner.

BONK!

Games like SPUD, DODGE BALL, and any other games where the ball is thrown at the player should be played with a playground ball or a gym ball. Throw the ball gently, directly at your target, and always below the person's waist. Don't let anyone in your group throw the ball hard. If the ball stings, then it is too hard and the thrower is out for that game. If it happens again, the person is out for good!

FIVE HUNDRED

So easy and oh-so-much fun!

* **PLAYERS:** 5 to 15
* **AGES:** 8 and up
* **SITE:** Outdoors or in a large indoor space like a gym
* **MATERIALS:** Playground or gym ball
* **GOAL:** To be the first person to get 500 points

Let's Play

The setup: One person is "It," and everyone else stands tossing distance away from him. "It" throws the ball in the air toward everyone else and calls a number between 50 and 500, saying something like *Who wants 200?*

Rules/scoring:

* If you catch the ball, you get as many points as "It" yelled. If you drop the ball, though, you lose the same number of points, (giving you a *negative* (minus) score.

* The Catcher becomes the next "It."

To win: The first person to get 500 points becomes "It" for the next game.

KIDS SPEAK!

All of us love to play FLINCH, FIVE HUNDRED, and SPUD! They are easy, we always end up laughing (especially with FLINCH), and everyone feels good, because these games are not really competitive. We think these are three games that make playing ball fun even for those who aren't exactly superstar athletes.

— Summer kids at Cedar Beach in Vermont

Great Games!

FLINCH

This is a game of quick reflexes, good observational skills, and nerves of steel. One nice kid I met told me he hated to be tickled, but he loved FLINCH, because he thought FLINCH was like being tickled — without any of the tickling! I think I get what he meant.

* **PLAYERS:** Large group — the more, the better — up to about 30 is fine
* **AGES:** 8 and up
* **SITE:** In a large yard; paved, or dirt area; or in a gym
* **MATERIALS:** Pinky or playground ball
* **GOAL:** To be the last one still in the game, or, if you are the Tosser, to get everyone out

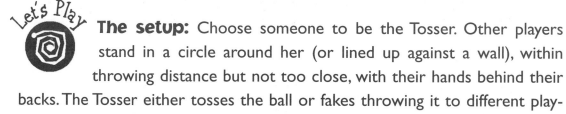

Let's Play

The setup: Choose someone to be the Tosser. Other players stand in a circle around her (or lined up against a wall), within throwing distance but not too close, with their hands behind their backs. The Tosser either tosses the ball or fakes throwing it to different players in the group.

Rules/scoring:

* If the Tosser actually throws the ball to you, you must catch it. If you miss, you are out and leave the circle.

* If the Tosser fakes the throw to you, you may not flinch or make any move indicating that you thought the ball would be thrown. If you flinch on a fake throw, you are out.

To win: The player who is last to be in becomes the Tosser for the next game.

Play Ball!

●TARGET!

This game, which is similar in some ways to UP AGAINST (page 18) helps you improve your aim, rather than just trying to hit the wall. Draw your targets in a size that is challenging for all, but still fun for all, too!

* **PLAYERS:** 1 to 6

* **AGES:** 8 and up

* **SITE:** Against a wall or chimney

* **MATERIALS:** Pinky or tennis ball, white chalk (ask permission to draw with chalk)

* **GOAL:** To hit the targets with the highest scores

* **TYKES:** You can draw big targets close to the ground, or even on the ground for rolling instead of throwing the ball

* **NOTE:** All targets don't have to be equally difficult; hardest targets have the highest point values

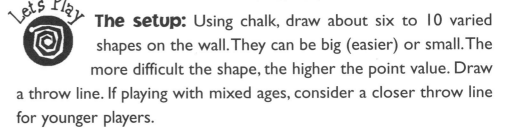

The setup: Using chalk, draw about six to 10 varied shapes on the wall. They can be big (easier) or small. The more difficult the shape, the higher the point value. Draw a throw line. If playing with mixed ages, consider a closer throw line for younger players.

The play: Standing behind the throw line, the player throws the ball so that it will bounce once, hit a target (shape) on the wall, and then, the player must catch the ball. If playing with others, take turns after each toss or decide that each player plays until a miss.

Rules/scoring: If you step over the throw line, the ball doesn't bounce before hitting the wall, or you don't catch the returning ball without a bounce, your turn is over and you don't score.

To win: Highest score wins.

Variations: There are so many variations to this game, that I'll mention just a few that we use, and you can make up more.

✳ *Orders:* You number the shapes and must play them in numerical order. If you hit a target that is not next, you don't score and/or you are out.

✳ *Call target:* Either you or another player calls the target for you. If you miss or hit the wrong target, you don't score and/or you are out. Some play that you draw the number of the target out of a hat for each turn. That way it is strictly by chance.

✳ *Outs:* You can play that you are out of the game (rather than just giving up your turn) when you make any of the misses listed in the rules (page 92).

✳ *No bouncies:* You throw directly at the wall and must hit the target and catch the return ball without the ball bouncing.

✳ *Bull's-eye:* By adding a bull's-eye in the center of each target, you make the game more difficult. If you hit a bull's-eye, add five points to your target's point value.

SLAPBALL

This is the street version of HANDBALL and can be played against a wall, chimney, or backboard near a tennis court. (If playing on a tennis court, please wear shoes that have white rubber soles. Otherwise, you may ruin the court's surface.)

* **PLAYERS:** 2 make a great one-on-one game; otherwise go to 4 or 6 (3 doesn't work as well)

* **AGES:** 10 and up

* **SITE:** Against a wall, chimney, tennis backboard, or steps — away from the road or any traffic

* **MATERIALS:** Pinky, tennis, or smaller handball with a glove (page 95)

* **GOAL:** To be the last one still in the game by throwing hard-to-slap or hard-to-catch balls or, if you are keeping score, the one with the highest score

* **NOTE:** A regulation handball is smaller and also harder, so it's best used with a glove, away from windows or young kids

Let's Play

The setup: "It," also called the Batter or Server, stands about 10 to 12 feet (3 to 3.5 m) away from the wall. All other players stand behind her. A back boundary is set about 20 feet (6 m) away from the wall.

The play: "It" stands in the front row and tosses the ball quite hard against the wall, aiming for the point where the wall meets the ground. The other player tries to slap the ball back against where the wall and the pavement meet after one bounce, while also moving into the front row position. After the first hit, the players set up a kind of rhythm, moving forward, slapping, and moving back.

Rules:

✳ With more than two players, call for the ball by saying *I got it!* if you are going to slap it.

✳ If you slap and miss, you are out.

✳ If you are the Batter and the ball goes out-of-bounds, you are out.

✳ If you are the Batter and the ball is good, but no one slaps it, you get a free pass that allows you to swing and miss once, but stay in the game. Batters can accumulate any number of free passes.

✳ If playing with three or more people, you can only slap the ball twice in a row.

✳ If you attempt to hog the ball (three slaps in a row), you are out.

Variations:

WALL BALL: You catch the ball after each slap. If you try to catch and miss, you are out, and the Batter gets a point. If you catch the ball, you get a point and the Batter is out; you become the next Batter. If no one catches a fair ball, the Batter gets a point and bats again.

STOOPBALL: A very popular game because you don't need a wall — just a stoop or set of porch stairs that isn't too close to a road. This can be played just like SLAPBALL or WALL BALL, only your target is the stair, bouncing the ball off the step and the riser above it. Best played by two, but can be played with four to six, either slapping and batting, or slapping and catching.

THIS IS A CERTIFIED, ALL-AMERICAN HANDBALL GLOVE.

THIS IS AN OLD WASHCLOTH.

Sam says: The best and easiest way to play any of these slap-the-ball games is to keep your hand wide open and swat the ball with your palm. Some people prefer to make a fist and punch the ball, but because a fist has less surface area than an open hand, I don't think that is a good alternative. Be sure to use your whole arm when swinging, because if you just slap using your wrist, the ball won't go very far. For the most difficult to retrieve shots, take careful aim to try to slap the ball directly at the line between the wall and the ground.

If you play this a lot, like we do, then you might want to buy a handball glove to protect your hand. Or, you can take an old washcloth and fold it the long way in thirds. Then wrap it around your open palm and fasten it with a rubber band or a big safety pin (on the top of your hand).

CATS GET A CORNER

This is just plain fun, no two ways about it. Find me a group of fun-loving people and I'll find you some cool cats to play this game. We always play that you can run in any direction — even diagonally — to reach a corner, which probably makes it a little bit too wild for some, but we think it is fun and funny.

* **PLAYERS:** 8 or more, but best with 12 to 20
* **AGES:** 8 and up
* **SITE:** Outdoors, in a large marked-off square; or indoors in a gym
* **MATERIALS:** Playground or gym balls, enough for several "Its" if playing with a big group
* **GOAL:** To be the last Cat to get tagged, or to be the "It" with the most tagged players

Let's Play

The setup:

1. Players mark off boundaries, making a big square or rectangle, large enough to really run in. The larger the square the better; otherwise, it is not a challenge for the Cats or the "Its."

2. Players decide how many "Its" there will be, depending on the number of players. Usually one "It" for every four or five players works well. All "Its" get a ball.

3. Another player is chosen to be the Caller (she can be a Cat and the Caller at the same time). The rest of the players (the Cats) pick different corners to stand in.

The play: To begin, the Caller yells, *Cats get a corner!* Each Cat takes off running for another corner. While the Cats are running, the "Its" in the center, try to tag one Cat each with a ball. The game continues according to the rules with the Caller yelling again.

Rules/scoring:

* Cats can run in any direction they choose — clockwise, counterclockwise, or diagonally across the area — as long as they are headed for a corner.

* Cats that are tagged by the ball are out.

* Some play that if you get tagged by a ball, you are a prisoner and stand in the middle alongside the "It" who tagged you. If a ball gets loose in play, a prisoner can grab it and toss it at another Cat. If the Cat is hit by the ball, the prisoner in the middle is free to return to a corner, and the newly tagged Cat becomes "It." The original "It" now is a prisoner alongside the new "It."

To win: The "It" with the most Cats at the end is the winner.

Variation: Running can be done in a clockwise direction, with everyone running in the same direction, which is best if the group has any kids younger than age 7.

KEEP AWAY

This is one of those games that is actually a lot more fun than it sounds. Want proof? Ask how many of your friends like playing this game. Then, get to it and play ball!

* **PLAYERS:** Large groups!

* **AGES:** 10 and up

* **SITE:** Outdoors in a yard or park, or inside a large gym

* **MATERIALS:** Pinky, tennis, or beach ball; one team needs to be identifiable, by wearing caps, armbands, or whatever

* **GOAL:** To keep the ball away from the other team by catching it, and to get the most points for your team

Let's Play

The setup:

1. Players agree on the boundaries and how long the game will go on. They divide into two easily identifiable teams. Each player pairs with a player from the opposite team (one-on-one formation similar to basketball), trying to form pairs of similarly sized players.

2. One player tosses the ball between two other players (a jump ball in basketball). Each player in the pair tries to catch it and throw it to one of his team members, keeping it away (aha!) from the other team's players.

HaTS VS. No HaTS

Ready?

Great Games!

HEY! NO FAIR!

Rules/scoring:

* If you are caught running with the ball, you are out. If you push to catch the ball, you are out.

* If two players catch the ball at the same time, a third player tosses it up between them, just like the "jump ball" used to start the game.

* If you step out-of-bounds to catch the ball, the catch doesn't count.

* Teams score one point each time they complete a pass to one of their team's players.

To win: The team with the most points after an agreed-upon time wins.

Variation:

MONKEY IN THE MIDDLE: Players form a line. The end players toss the ball back and forth over the other Monkeys in the middle. The Monkeys try to jump up and intercept the ball. If a Monkey catches the ball, he switches places with the player who threw it. This is a lot of fun played at the beach or in a pool. And, in the winter, play this with a ball (not a snowball) in deep snow. You'll be surprised at how much more difficult it is in lots of snow.

DODGE BALL

BEACH DODGE BALL, TEAM DODGE BALL, FREE-FOR-ALL DODGE BALL, CIRCLE DODGE BALL, LINE DODGE BALL— the one thing all of these games have in common is that someone is trying to dodge a ball tossed at him. To be sure, the winner is the one who is an artful dodger!

* **PLAYERS:** 8 or more

* **AGES:** 8 and up

* **SITE:** Large space outdoors or in a gym

* **MATERIALS:** Playground or gym ball

* **GOAL:** To eliminate the players from the other team (in TEAM DODGE BALL) and avoid being eliminated yourself

* **TYKES:** Lots of DODGE BALL games can be played by rolling the ball at someone's feet, which is loads of fun for tykes

Let's Play

FOR TEAM DODGE BALL

The setup: Draw a line down the center of the playing area to divide it into two courts. Players divide evenly into two teams, and stand on opposite sides of the line. Decide which team gets to go first. One player from the first team throws the ball at any player or group of players on the other team. (You don't need a specific target.)

Rules/scoring:

* If the ball hits a player, he is out of the game.

* If a player catches the ball, the Thrower is out of the game. The Catcher throws the ball back, trying to tag another player on the opposing team.

* If no one is hit and the ball isn't caught, any player near the ball can pick it up, toss the ball, and continue the game.

* Always aim the ball so it hits players below the waist. Players may dodge the ball by moving, running, jumping, or ducking to avoid being hit.

* If you step over the centerline or out-of-bounds at any time, you are out of the game.

To win: The team that tags all the other players with the ball, or the team that has the most players left after an agreed-upon time wins.

Variations:

FREE-FOR-ALL DODGE BALL: This is my favorite form of dodge ball and my guess is that it is the original game. Here "It" gets the ball and tosses it gently at anyone (or at a group of players). If a person is hit, he is out. If someone catches the ball, the Thrower is out. If the ball is free, anyone can pick it up after it touches the ground. She then throws the ball, trying to get someone else out. Last one standing wins. To make this extra hard, play in a small gym or basement so the ball can also bounce off the walls. If you are hit by a back-bounce, you are out.

CIRCLE DODGE BALL: Like the team version (page 100 to 101), only here the Throwers form a circle around the Dodgers instead of playing on two courts. The Throwers gently throw the ball at the Dodgers. Once everyone is out, the players switch places, with the Throwers becoming Dodgers.

PRISONER DODGE BALL: Players who are eliminated in TEAM DODGE BALL go to a "jail" at the back of each team's court. If a player on your team throws a ball to the jail and you catch it, you can get out of jail and rejoin the game. If you are in jail and drop the throw after touching it, the Thrower must go to jail, too. Some versions play that if the throw hits an agreed-upon target (such as a nearby basketball hoop), everyone on that team gets to be freed from jail.

KICKBALL

Along with SPUD (pages 88 to 89), this ranks right up there at the top for ball games. It can be played by kids of all ages (including the 'rents), you don't need any great ball-playing ability, and everyone gets to experience some team spirit! It has the same sort of rules as baseball, softball, and stickball, but it is played with a larger playground ball.

* **PLAYERS:** Ideally at least 14

* **AGES:** 7 and up

* **SITE:** Outside in a yard or park

* **MATERIALS:** A kickball or playground ball; something to mark home plate and the bases (like an old piece of carpet or a bath mat)

* **NOTE:** Even though the person on the pitcher's mound is called the "pitcher," she is not pitching or throwing as in baseball or softball. Instead, she rolls the ball fast, steady, and hard to home plate.

Let's Play

The setup:

1. Mark out a baseball diamond on the ground, with about 30 feet (9 m) between bases. Mark the three bases, home plate, and the pitching mound.

2. Divide into even teams, and decide which team is kicking and which is on the field first (a coin toss — heads or tails — works well).

3. Players in the field take positions to cover the bases and, if enough players, to cover the outfield, too. One person pitches and one person is the Catcher.

4. Each team decides on its order of kickers, using all players before anyone can kick again.

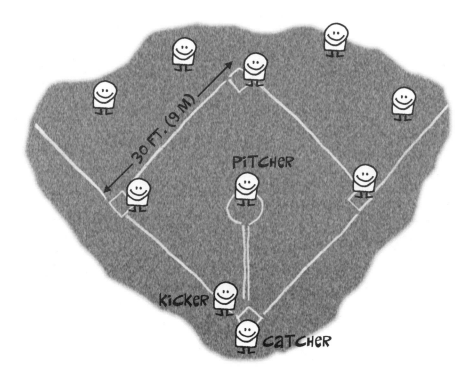

30 FT. (9 M)

PITCHER

KICKER

CATCHER

Play Ball!

The play:

1. The Pitcher rolls the ball to the first Kicker at home plate, who kicks the ball into the field and runs to first base. Players may run to more than one base, or even all the way to home plate, on one kick, if possible. Each run to home plate scores as one point.

2. Kickers continue kicking the ball in turn, loading up the bases, and running to home plate, until the team gets three outs. Then the teams switch places, with the Kickers taking positions on the field and the Fielders kicking.

Rules/scoring:

✳ If the Kicker misses the ball, it is a *strike*. Three strikes and the Kicker is *out*. The player who kicked the *out* goes to the end of the line of Kickers.

✳ If the ball goes outside the *foul lines* (the lines connecting the first and third bases to home plate), it is a *foul*. The Kicker gets to kick again. The first two fouls are counted as strikes, and any additional fouls are not counted.

✳ If the Pitcher rolls the ball high, or off course, it counts as a *ball*. Four balls means the Kicker gets to walk to the first base, and the player on first base moves to second.

✳ If a player in the field catches a kicked ball before it hits the ground, or tags the base before a runner gets there, it counts as an *out*. Any player who is *out* goes to the back of the kicking line.

✳ If the Kicker is tagged by the ball while running to base, she is *out*. Any other players tagged by the ball while running between bases are *out*.

✳ Players already on base may *steal bases* by running to the next base before the kick (after the roll begins), but if they are tagged by the ball, they are *out*.

To win: The team with the most runs after each team has the same number of turns kicking is the winner.

Kicker   Kicker   Distance-Kicker   Kicker   Kicker   Distance-Kicker

KIDS SPEAK! The most important strategy in kickball involves the order of the kickers. The distance-kickers should be placed every third person in the kicking order. Then, when the other kickers get on base, the distance-kickers may be able to "kick" them home to score. I'm not great at kicking either close in or far out, so I suppose that is why it's easier for me to see the importance of a team kicking strategy. But, I'm really good at third base.

— David

Multicultural Games

You know, some days I wake up and I am just so glad to be me! I hope that happens to you, too. On those days I find myself glad I know so many people who come from other parts of the world, or whose parents or grandparents grew up in other countries. It's fun, it's interesting, it makes life nicer and richer when we are welcomed into each other's homes, enjoying being friends and neighbors.

But, back to games! It seems that with games there is really nothing new under the sun. Many of our favorite "modern" games are as old as the hills, which is to say very, very old, which is to say ancient, which is to say thousands of years old!

So, let's take a look at some of the games that started in one place and have ended up in a lot of other places! And while we are at it, here's something I've been wondering about: If kids all over the world like to play the same kinds of games, doesn't that mean that people all over the world start out the same — curious, fun-loving, imaginative, and just plain liking to spend time with each other?

Sam says: To choose who goes first, or teams, please see pages 12 to 16. For additional ball, board, and tag games, please see the index.

SENAT

This ancient Egyptian board game is the great-great-great-great grandfather of CHECKERS (page 44). We aren't certain precisely how the game was played, but we do know the object of SENAT, which means "passing," is the same as CHECKERS — to capture the other player's pieces.

In SENAT, the pieces are called *kelb,* and the squares are called *ooyen,* or "eyes." The Egyptians sat on the floor and played on a low table.

* **PLAYERS:** 2 (see note, below)

* **AGES:** 8 and up

* **SITE:** Anywhere

* **MATERIALS:** Square piece of stiff cardboard, ruler, black marker or felt-tip pen; 2 sets of 12 checkers, or pebbles marked with paint or nail polish in sets of 12

* **GOAL:** To capture the most kelb

* **NOTE:** Since you make the board and the playing pieces, you can easily have several games going at once when you have a larger group. Then have playoffs with the winners.

Let's Play

The setup:

1. To make the board, draw 25 squares, or ooyen, on the cardboard by drawing four lines in both directions. Mark an X in the center square.

2. Choose who goes first. That player places two kelb anywhere on the board, except on the middle ooyen, which is left empty until the game begins. Then, the other player places two kelb. The players continue to take turns until all the pieces are on the board.

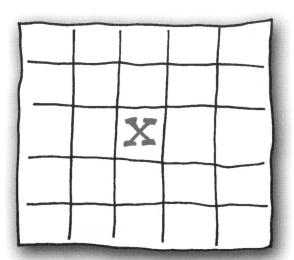

The play:

1. To begin playing, the first player moves a kelb onto the middle (X) space, signifying the honor of being first.

2. Kelb can be moved one space forward, backward, or sideways per turn. They cannot jump or move diagonally.

Rules/scoring:

✳ Kelb are captured (and removed) when the other player traps you between two of his pieces. But, if you purposely move between two of your opponent's pieces, your kelb cannot be taken. We play that in this case you have to say *before* you move, *Kelb is visiting.* Otherwise, we assume that you moved by mistake and your kelb can be captured.

✳ When you capture a kelb, take another turn, and keep on taking turns as long as you capture kelb.

✳ If you cannot move, you lose your turn, but the other player has to open up a space for your next move.

To win: The game is over when a player cannot move, or has no kelb left. The winner is the player with the most captured kelb.

KIDS SPEAK!

There are a lot of strategies once you get into this game (SENAT). The most important thing is to place your kelb along the edges of the board when you are starting, as that will give you the best chances of moving in for the capture, while protecting your kelb.

— Sarah R.

Make American Indian Playing Pieces

Along with SENAT, there are many other games where you make your own playing pieces, using buttons, pebbles that you color code, or small sets of shells. The American Indians of the California Sierra foothills, the Sierra Miwok, in the U.S.A. made these beautiful playing pieces. They probably were used with a particular game and made from black walnuts filled with charcoal-darkened pitch. The Iroquois Nation, in what is now New York State, played a similar game, using plum stones (pits) that were painted dark on one side.

These are so beautiful that you might want to make a set for your game-playing friends!

Materials: 6 walnut shell halves, nail, sandpaper, clay or wax (wax from cheese wrapping is perfect). Plus small shell fragments, pebbles, sea glass, or seed beads.

Here's how: With the nail, pick out any walnut meat still in the shell. Sand the shells to smooth out any sharp edges. Fill the indentation with wax or clay, pressing to flatten the top. Decorate the filling with shell pieces, tiny pebbles, sea glass, or seed beads.

MANCALA

Kids of all ages have been playing MANCALA around the world for thousands of years! In Africa, where MANCALA originated, kids use pebbles to play on a game-playing surface made by scooping out shallow holes in the ground. You can make a super mancala board with an empty egg carton. Or, you can make a really nice hand-carved game board from a piece of chunk balsa wood, available at craft stores. And, there are mancala games for sale in stores, too. Whichever board you use, be sure to have fun playing the ancients' way.

* **PLAYERS:** 2
* **AGES:** All ages
* **SITE:** Anywhere
* **MATERIALS:** You can play the traditional African way, or make your own game board from an egg carton; 48 pebbles, dried beans, or marbles
* **GOAL:** To move the most stones into your mancala bin
* **NOTE:** Be sure to keep playing pieces away from toddlers, who could swallow them and choke. Thank you.

The setup:

1. To make an egg-carton board, cut the lid of an egg carton in half, and tape or staple one piece onto each end of the eggcups. For playing pieces, gather 48 pebbles, use dried beans, or make your own playing pieces (page 109).

2. Place the board between two players. Put four playing pieces in each of the 12 eggcups, leaving the two "mancala bins" on the ends empty. Your playing cups are the six in front of you; your mancala bin is the one on your right.

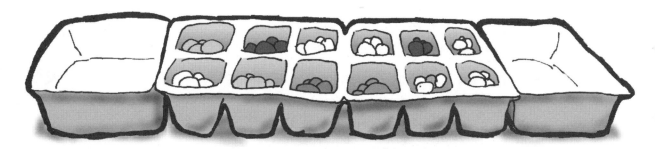

Mancala Bin └────── **Cups** ──────┘ **Mancala Bin**

The play: Decide who goes first. To take a turn, pick up all the stones in any one of your cups, and drop them, one by one in a counter-clockwise direction, into each of the next four cups around the board. If you pass your mancala bin, drop a stone in, but don't drop one into the other player's mancala bin (just skip over it). Keep taking turns placing the stones in one cup at a time.

Rules/scoring:

✳ If the last of your stones on your turn falls in your mancala bin, take another turn.

✳ If the last stone on your turn falls in one of your empty cups, put all the stones from your opponent's cup directly across from your empty cup, plus the capturing stone, into your mancala bin.

✳ If you touch the stones in one of your cups (to count them, for example), then you must play them.

To win: The game ends when one player runs out of stones in his individual cups. The other player gets to place any remaining stones left in her cups into her mancala bin. The player with the most stones in his own mancala bin wins.

GO BANANAS!

String stories and games have been around for a very long time! After all, there have always been tall grasses, reeds, and vines to use instead of string. Try this string game for fun, and remember that African kids play with string — and eat bananas just like you do!

* **PLAYERS:** 1
* **AGES:** 10 and up
* **SITE:** Anywhere, anytime; good when traveling
* **MATERIALS:** 6 feet (2 m) of string

Let's Play

1. Knot the string so that it makes a big loop. Wrap the loop around the thumb and pinky of your right hand. The top of the loop should rest on the palm of your hand.

2. Hook your left pointer over the string on your right palm. Pull it all the way down.

3. Again, hook your left pointer over the string on your right palm and pull it all the way down.

4. Now for the trickiest step: Stick your left palm against your right palm, with the string resting between your pinky and ring finger and between your pointer and thumb. Stick your left pinky into the loop below your right pinky and stick your left thumb into the loop below your right thumb.

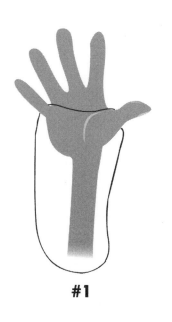

#1

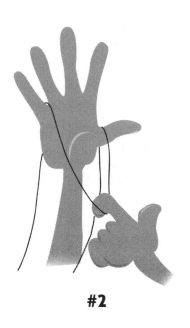

#2

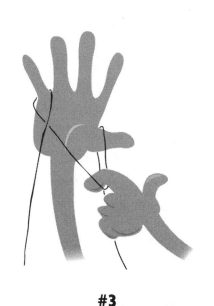

#3

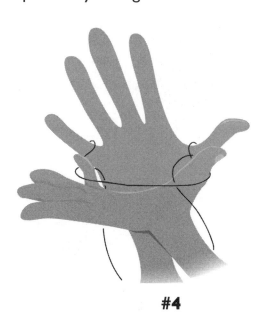

#4

5. Pull your left pinky and thumb down and through the hanging loops.

6. Pull the loops all the way down.

7. Drop the three middle fingers on your right hand into the three holes, as shown.

8. Turn your hand so that your palm is facing up. Then, gently pull the top string as far as it can go.

9. Now you should have four bananas hanging on a string. Let go of the four loops around your right hand. Hang onto the string in your left hand. Then, have a friend pick a banana out of the bunch!

Sam says: If you are anything like me — all thumbs — string tricks can be a real challenge until you get the knack of it. I used to have the worst time figuring this stuff out, but I got pretty good at it eventually. I found it much easier having someone show me than trying to figure it out. My sister Jane can do these so fast that it is amazing to watch.

Ask some adults what string stories and tricks they used to do, as these have been around "forever." Be sure to have someone show you CAT'S CRADLE if you are having trouble getting started. That's the one I learned on.

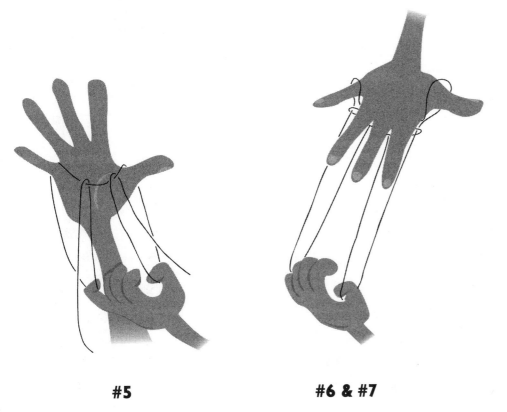

#5　　　　**#6 & #7**

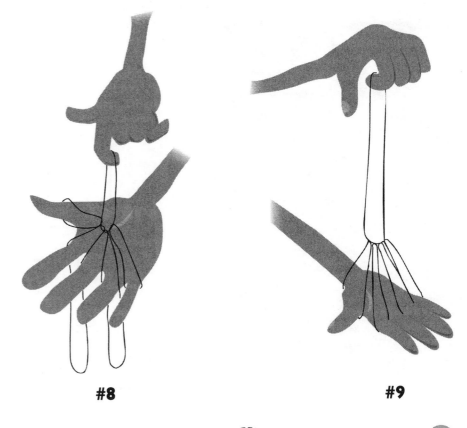

#8　　　　**#9**

NINE MEN'S MORRIS

This is one of the oldest board games from anywhere in the world. A very early example of the board was found in an Egyptian temple built around 1400 B.C., which is about 3,400 years ago! Now here is what I hope you can tell me: How did such an old game stay around from then — or even earlier! — through the Middle Ages when it became popular again, and travel through time and space so kids still play it today? Can you shed some light on that for me, please?

* **PLAYERS:** 2
* **AGES:** 10 and up
* **SITE:** Anywhere; also fun to draw and play on the beach
* **MATERIALS:** Stiff paper, ruler, marker; 18 playing pieces (9 per player) of 2 distinct patterns or colors (use checkers, buttons, colored pieces of paper)
* **GOAL:** To remove your opponent's pieces so he only has two pieces

Let's Play

The play:

1. Choose who goes first. Then take turns placing pieces on the board on the *points,* which is wherever lines intersect (see the dots).

2. Be sure to place your pieces so they can move easily; don't bunch them up in one area. The more directions a piece can move, the better the placement (you must move along the lines to the next point). Notice that at the midpoints of the *middle* square, you can move your pieces in four directions, but also note that in the corners you can only move in two directions.

3. The object is to form a *mill,* or three pieces in a row.

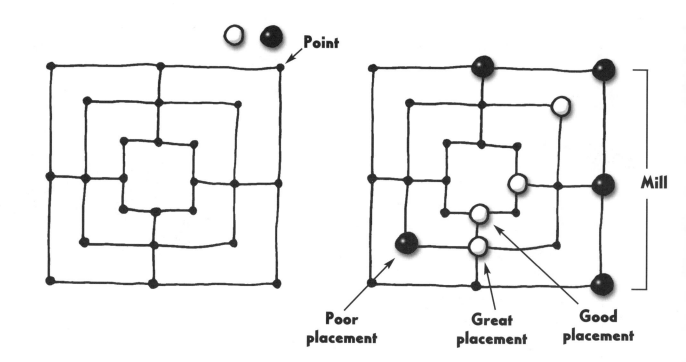

Point

Poor placement

Great placement

Good placement

Mill

Rules/scoring:

✳ After all the pieces are on the board, players continue to try to make mills by moving their pieces. A piece can move only to one point at a time along a line. No jumping is permitted.

✳ You can make a mill horizontally, vertically, or diagonally.

✳ Whenever you make a mill, you remove one of your opponent's pieces that is not part of a mill from the board. (You may take a piece from her mill *only* if there are no other available pieces.)

✳ If one piece is removed from one of your mills on one turn and you replace it on your next turn, you make a new mill with all of its benefits (such as removing your opponent's piece)!

To win: When one player has only two pieces remaining on the board, the other player is the winner. Or, if no one can move, the player with the most pieces on the board wins.

KiDS SPEAK! How do I win so many games? It is always a matter of strategies. Lots of board games appear easy, but if you find a strategy that works, then use it to full advantage. The kid who just plays by reacting is always on the defensive, but play a good offensive game and you'll be a winner.

—Dan

ALQUERQUE

Alquerque (ahl-CARE-kay) is the Spanish name for an ancient board game that originated in the Middle East. Played by two players, it's one of many games we've already played where you capture your opponent's playing pieces by jumping.

* **PLAYERS:** 2
* **AGES:** 10 and up
* **SITE:** Indoors
* **MATERIALS:** Poster board, ruler, marker; 2 sets of 12 playing pieces each with sets easily distinguishable (use checkers, buttons, or colored pieces of paper)
* **GOAL:** To capture your opponent's playing pieces

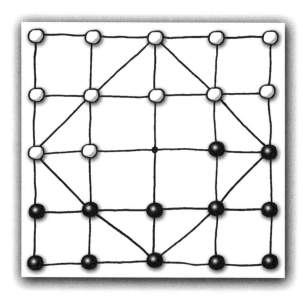

 The setup:

1. Draw the board [12 inches (30 cm) square] as shown on poster board, cardboard, or stiff paper. Fill in the dots at the intersections.

2. Place your playing pieces on the intersections of the first two rows facing you and on the two right-hand intersections of the middle row.

The play: The play is much like CHECKERS, with two big exceptions: You move on the lines, landing on the intersections, not on the spaces. And players can move in any direction right from the beginning.

Rules/scoring:

* Decide who goes first. Players take turns moving pieces along the lines one intersection at a time in any direction, trying to capture the opponent's pieces by jumping over them.

* You may make multiple jumps in varied directions.

* You *must* jump (and thus capture) your opponent's pieces whenever there's an opportunity; otherwise, your opponent takes your playing piece.

To win: The winner is the first to capture all of her opponent's pieces.

 Great Games!

TANGRAMS

TANGRAMS is more a puzzle than a game, but it is so old and so much fun that I had to include it. The Chinese call it *Qi Qiao Ban* (chee cheeow bahn) which means "the seven clever pieces." A man reportedly named Tan invented it many thousands of years ago in China.

The reason that TANGRAMS are so fascinating to me is that they show an amazingly creative and inquisitive vision. Don't you wonder how Mr. Tan came up with something that appears so simple but is really so complex?

* **PLAYERS:** 2
* **AGES:** 8 and up
* **SITE:** Indoors on a flat surface
* **MATERIALS:** Pencil, tracing paper, scissors, cardboard
* **GOAL:** To arrange the seven pieces into a square or other recognizable shapes

Let's Play

The setup: These seven simple pieces that assemble into a square can be arranged to be any number of recognizable things. Try it by tracing this pattern and cutting out the shapes.

The play: Begin by rearranging the shapes into a square just to get a feel for where this is going. Then, arrange them into a bird, a duck, or a fish to get started. And keep going because there are 1,600 different shapes that can be made!

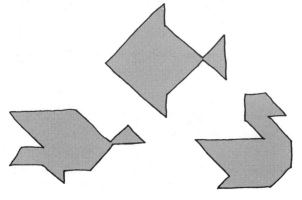

TIDDLYWINKS

This game, created in England, was mostly played by adults until it was mass-produced and the kids got hold of it. A casual game, it can be enjoyed as a nondemanding pastime, or you can play quite ferociously, if you get into a fun competition. We always played on a carpet, but keep in mind that if the carpet is too soft, the game is too easy. For more of a challenge, play on a stack of newspapers, as they have just enough "give" to keep the tiddlywinks flying by.

Official store-bought games come with a board with points, but we always make our own shooter lines and boundaries, and skip the points of the playing board.

* **PLAYERS:** 2 to 4 work best

* **AGES:** All ages

* **SITE:** Anyplace with desired surface with "give" (carpet, table-cloth, stack of newspapers, grass)

* **MATERIALS:** For *shooters*, each player needs a quarter; for *winks*, each player needs about 4 dimes with each person's set marked with a colored marker for easy identification. A small lid from a mayonnaise or jelly jar for the *cup*, and masking or duct tape.

* **GOAL:** To get all your winks in the cup, or to reach the target score first

* **TYKES:** Watch your winks and shooters if there are young children around who might put them in their mouths. For older tykes, play on a very soft surface with the cup fairly close by.

Let's Play

The setup: Use the masking tape to mark a shooter line on all four sides of the cup, about 16 inches (40 cm) away from the cup. (You can set the distance depending on the skill levels of the players.) Then mark the boundaries, usually about another foot (30 cm) beyond the shooting line.

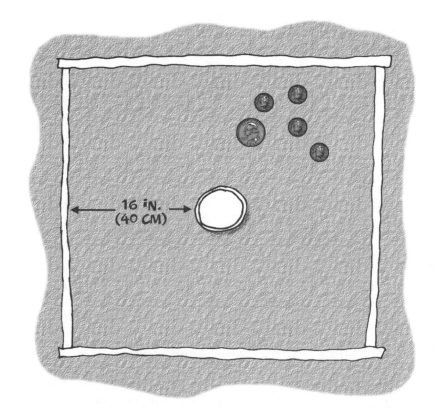

16 IN.
(40 CM)

Great Games!

 **Part of the fun of a game is knowing the best techniques and the lingo.** TIDDLYWINKS isn't particularly difficult, but the lingo sure is a hoot to me, and maybe it will be to you, too!

Shooter: The bigger piece (quarter in our game) in a real TIDDLYWINKS set that is used to press down on the wink

Wink: The smaller playing pieces (the dime in our game) is color coded in a set so each player has her own

Cup: This is a small glass dish (screw-on jar lids in our game) to receive the flying winks. Sometimes it is called the *pot*.

Squidge: The technique of pressing down with the shooter against the wink's edge and then releasing the pressure, causing the wink to flip high and wide, and land in the cup. The best squidging technique is to press hard and release completely, but you need to take into account the softness of the surface and the distance to and height of the cup.

Grass: Tufts of carpet that winks get caught on

Leaner: A wink that lands leaning against the cup's edge

Treading: When one player's wink lands on another player's wink

Strategies: Although it is in my nature to try for the cup on each turn, some say that it is better to move toward the cup in smaller increments, which gives you better control of your shooting. Also, you'll need to decide whether to tread on another player's wink, thereby momentarily placing it under your control, or to stay focused on your own game and winning. My own choice usually is to try to keep my own winks out of trouble.

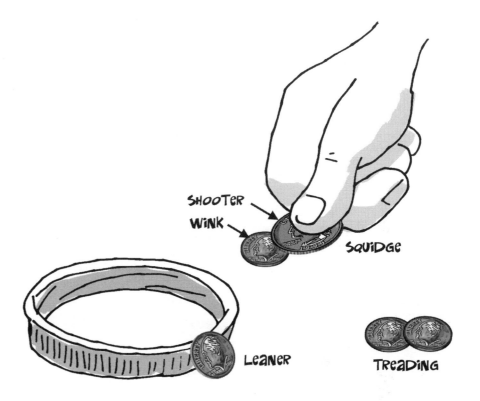

SHOOTER
WINK
SQUIDGE
LEANER
TREADING

The play: Each player sets a wink at the same starting line and squidges it using the shooter. The wink closest to the cup goes first, and then play continues clockwise, with all players squidging from their own shooter lines, or using one line for all.

Rules/scoring:

✳ The first player squidges the wink. If he gets it in the cup, then he goes again. If not, he leaves the wink where it is, unless the wink is out of bounds. In that case, the player must move it back to the shooter line. Play moves to the player on the left.

✳ On following turns, each player can either begin a new wink, or continue playing one that didn't make it in the cup.

✳ If a wink lands standing in the "grass," it must be moved back to the starting line for the player's *next* turn.

✳ Try to avoid having a wink land leaning against the cup. If it does, you have to knock it over with another wink (not an easy thing to do!). If the leaner is your last wink, then you may take one of your winks out of the cup, and beginning at the shooter line again, use it to dislodge the leaning wink. You must proceed to get both remaining winks in the cup.

✳ If your wink should land on someone else's wink, called treading, the other player must wait until you play your top wink before she can play her bottom wink, even if it means she has to skip her turn. Once the top wink is played, then she can play the bottom wink.

To win: The first player with all her winks in the cup is the winner.

Variations:

✳ Some play that each player has his own shooting line; others play that all players shoot from one line. The major difference is that if you all shoot from one line, you are more likely to tread on each other's winks.

✳ You can play with more winks per player, which makes the game not only longer, but also more exciting, as players need to use definite treading strategies.

Ball, Tag & other Active Games

Ready for a little more action? The games from other cultures are not all board games and intricate puzzles. People everywhere enjoy playing BALL, TAG, and other games of seeking and capture. So, you better begin warming up because here we go!

TRIGON

Sam & friends All-Time favorites

If you were a kid growing up in ancient Rome, you'd probably have a pet parrot and maybe a pet turtle or squirrel, too. You'd play BALL, TAG, and MARBLES, and, of course, none of your toys would need batteries! You'd likely have a swing, some beautiful dolls made of ivory or wood, and even play in pretend battles with little wooden soldiers. As you got older, you'd play BACKGAMMON. Not so different for around 700 to 500 B.C., or about 2,700 years ago! Is that as amazing to you as it is to me?

TRIGON is a wonderful ancient Roman game, played in a triangle with three players. And, in case you wondered, *tri* means "three" in Latin, the Roman language.

Let's Play

The setup: Mark off an *equilateral* triangle (all sides equal) about 20 feet (6 m) on each side. Each player stands at a point of the triangle. Players decide how they are scoring and throwing. One player tosses one ball at a time into play.

* **PLAYERS:** 3 at one time but more can hold a play-off or rotate in
* **AGES:** 8 and up
* **SITE:** Outdoors or in a gym; need a triangle 20 feet (6 m) on a side
* **MATERIALS:** 3 to 6 Pinky or tennis balls; white chalk, tape, or a stick to mark a triangle
* **GOAL:** To be the last player still catching
* **NOTE:** See the variation (page 122) for larger groups; younger kids may enjoy this game played with a playground ball

Rules/scoring:

✳ Play with three or more balls. The balls always move in the same direction.

✳ As you add the balls, pick up the pace until they are moving so quickly, you feel as if you are juggling.

✳ Some people play that you have to throw with your nondominant hand (righties throw with left; lefties throw with right).

✳ If a player drops the ball, he gets one miss against him.

✳ If a player throws a wild ball, far outside the range of the triangle, she gets a "miss." But, if a player manages to catch a wild ball, she gets a "save" and is allowed to subtract one miss (or put it in reserve if she doesn't have any misses yet).

✳ Ten misses and you are out of the game (or set your own number of misses allowed per person). Continue playing with two players until only one player is left.

To win: Last one left is the winner.

Variations:

PLAY-OFFS: When we have a larger group of players available, we play five misses, and you are out. We rotate a new player in each time someone gets to five misses. That ends up being a play-off of sorts, since the last three standing players will play to the end. Or, if there are enough balls available, you can have several games going at once and then hold a play-off. Either way, this is a lot of fun!

SWITCHEROO: This is a different take on TRIGON. Here you move *only one ball* quickly to each player. The complicating factor in SWITCHEROO is that any player with the ball can switch the ball's direction at any time, *without announcing it*. If the Catcher misses, the Thrower gets the point. Whoever gets 15 points first, is the winner. (In SWITCHEROO, you want to get points; in TRIGON, you don't want to get misses.)

TLACHTLI

Try this version of the traditional Mexican ball game TLACHTLI (TLOT-lee), which is still played during certain festivals in the states of Mayarit and Sinaloa on the west coast of Mexico. It is thought to resemble the ancient "game of the Gods," played first by the Olmec near the ruins of the Mexican pyramids. Back then, it was a deadly serious game with religious meaning and with the losers sometimes suffering death. (That sure doesn't sound like a game to me!)

* **PLAYERS:** At least 10 (enough to make 2 teams)
* **AGES:** 8 and up
* **SITE:** Outdoors (played by teams on a flat field divided into sections)
* **MATERIALS:** Beach ball, 2 trash cans
* **GOAL:** To be the first team to score 25 points

The setup: Mark off a rectangular area into two halves. Divide the group into even teams (page 16). Place a trash can at the center of each back line.

The play: Do a jump ball (page 98) on the centerline. Each team tries to pass the ball from player to player toward its goal (trash can), *without letting the ball hit the ground.* Players may use any part of their bodies *except* their hands to get the ball into their trash can.

Rules/scoring:

* The team scores five points each time the ball goes into its goal.
* If the ball hits the ground, or a player uses his hands to pass, the other team takes over at that spot.
* After each score, the play starts with a jump ball.

To win: The first team to score 25 points is the winner.

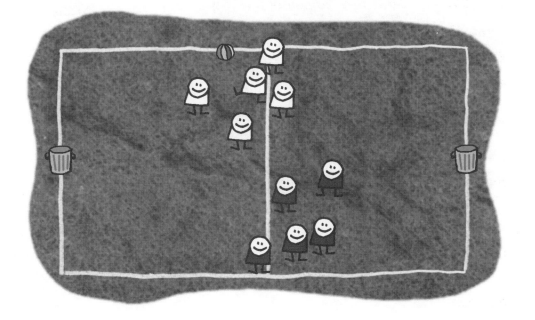

TAKING COCONUTS!
(VER VER ARAS LAMA)

This game, in its original version, in Papua, New Guinea, was played with coconuts, but if coconuts don't happen to grow on trees where you live, then balls work at least as well! This is about playing the game to its fullest, without the motivation that comes from competing! In fact, in the native Hanahan language of Papua, there isn't even a word for "winning," so play this one just for the fun of it!

* **PLAYERS:** 4
* **AGES:** 7 and up
* **SITE:** Outdoors/indoors in gym
* **MATERIALS:** Balls (or coconuts), a stick or white chalk to mark circles
* **GOAL:** To get three coconuts into your circle

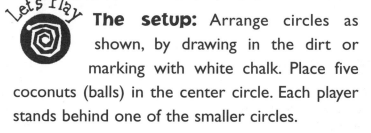

The setup: Arrange circles as shown, by drawing in the dirt or marking with white chalk. Place five coconuts (balls) in the center circle. Each player stands behind one of the smaller circles.

The play: Players try to *place* the coconuts (balls) — not *roll* them or *throw* them — one at a time in their own circle. They may take coconuts from the center circle and from each other, moving as quickly as they can. The game becomes a continuous movement of players and coconuts!

To win: The game ends when everyone is tired, thirsty, and laughing.

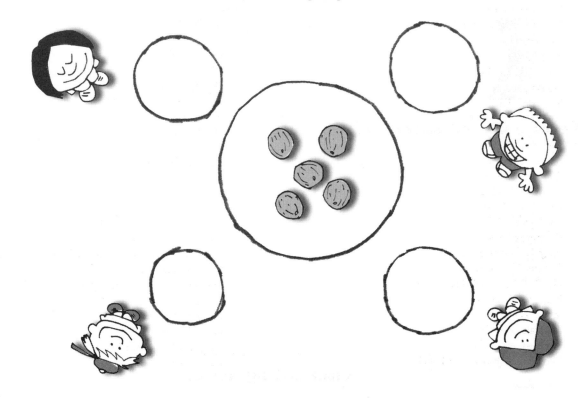

:Index:

SITES

Many of these games can be played in multiple sites. For example, word games can be played anywhere and so can board games. This listing tells you some of your choices when you are indoors or out, in a large or small space.

Indoors/Outdoors – nonactive games
Quiet games played without running or tossing balls, such as in a living room or on a small terrace or porch

Indoors – somewhat active games

Played in a basement or a playroom where no need to worry about breaking anything or disturbing others; permission needed to use white chalk in basement and toss ball against wall

Outdoors – active games for a small to mid-sized space

Games best played on a porch, sidewalk (away from traffic), grassy area, in a yard, or area around your home where balls can be tossed and you can use white chalk

Outdoors/Indoors – large outdoor space or gym

Games that usually are played on a ball field,

large outdoor playing area such as a park or several yards (with neighbors' permission), or indoors in a gym

NUMBERS OF PLAYERS

Some games are best played with a few players and some are best played when there are large groups. You can always improvise and, using the number of players available, come up with your own rules, so that you either have play-offs or rotate in. No need for teams to be even, because these are games, not big competitions.

One player

Only two players

127

¡More Good Books from Williamson Publishing!

American Bookseller Pick of the Lists
Parents' Choice Approved
SUMMER FUN!
60 Activities for a Kid-Perfect Summer
by Susan Williamson, $12.95

The Kids' Book of
INCREDIBLY FUN CRAFTS
by Roberta Gould, $14.95

KIDS' EASY BIKE CARE
Tune-Ups, Tools & Quick Fixes
by Steve Cole, $8.95

YO-YO!
Tips & Tricks from a Pro
by Ron Burgess, $8.95

Parents' Choice Gold Award
Benjamin Franklin Best Juvenile Nonfiction Award
KIDS MAKE MUSIC!
Clapping and Tapping from Bach to Rock
by Avery Hart and Paul Mantell, $12.95

BE A CLOWN!
Techniques from a Real Clown
by Ron Burgess, $8.95

Dr. Toy 10 Best Socially Responsible Products
MAKE YOUR OWN BIRDHOUSES & FEEDERS
by Robyn Haus, $8.95

40 KNOTS TO KNOW
Hitches, Loops, Bends & Bindings
by Emily Stetson, $8.95

GARDEN FUN!
Indoors & Out; In Pots & Small Spots
by Vicky Congdon, $8.95

Parents' Choice Approved
BAKE THE BEST-EVER COOKIES!
by Sarah A. Williamson, $8.95

Selection of Book-of-the-Month Club
KIDS COOK!
Fabulous Food for the Whole Family
by Sarah Williamson and Zachary Williamson, $12.95

Parents' Choice Recommended
ALMOST-INSTANT SCRAPBOOKS
by Laura Check, $8.95

Parents' Choice Recommended
PAPER-FOLDING FUN!
50 Awesome Crafts to Weave, Twist & Curl
by Ginger Johnson, $12.95

MAKE YOUR OWN COOL CARDS
40 Awesome Notes & Invitations!
by Peg Blanchette & Terri Thibault, $8.95

KIDS' EASY KNITTING PROJECTS
by Peg Blanchette, $8.95

Parents' Choice Recommended
Independent Publisher Book Award
The Kids' Guide to FIRST AID
Bruises, Burns, Stings, Sprains & Other Ouches
by Karen Buhler Gale, R.N., $12.95

ForeWord Magazine Book of the Year Finalist
DRAWING HORSES (that look real!)
by Don Mayne, $8.95

Oppenheim Toy Portfolio Gold Award
DRAW YOUR OWN CARTOONS!
by Don Mayne, $8.95

Parents' Choice Approved
BOREDOM BUSTERS!
The Curious Kids' Activity Book
by Avery Hart and Paul Mantell, $12.95

KIDS MAKE MAGIC!
The Complete Guide to Becoming an Amazing Magician
by Ron Burgess, $12.95

Parents' Choice Recommended
EASY ART FUN!
Do-It-Yourself Crafts for Beginning Readers
by Jill Frankel Hauser, $12.95

Parents' Choice Gold Award
FUN WITH MY 5 SENSES
Activities to Build Learning Readiness
by Sarah A. Williamson, $12.95

MAKE YOUR OWN CHRISTMAS ORNAMENTS
by Ginger Johnson, $8.95

THE KIDS' BOOK OF
MULTICULTURAL CRAFTS
by Roberta Gould, $12.95

Create a WILDLIFE HABITAT
for Urban & Suburban Small Spaces
by Emily Stetson, $8.95

Parents' Choice Recommended
THE KIDS' BOOK OF WEATHER FORECASTING
Build a Weather Station, "Read" the Sky & Make Predictions!
by meteorologist Mark Breen, $12.95

Parents' Choice Gold Award
Dr. Toy Best Vacation Product
THE KIDS' NATURE BOOK
365 Indoor/Outdoor Activities & Experiences
by Susan Milord, $12.95

Parents' Choice Recommended
Orbus Pictus Award for Outstanding Nonfiction
KIDS' ART WORKS!
Creating with Color, Design, Texture & More
by Sandi Henry, $12.95

American Bookseller Pick of the Lists
RAINY DAY PLAY!
Explore, Create, Discover, Pretend
by Nancy Fusco Castaldo, $12.95